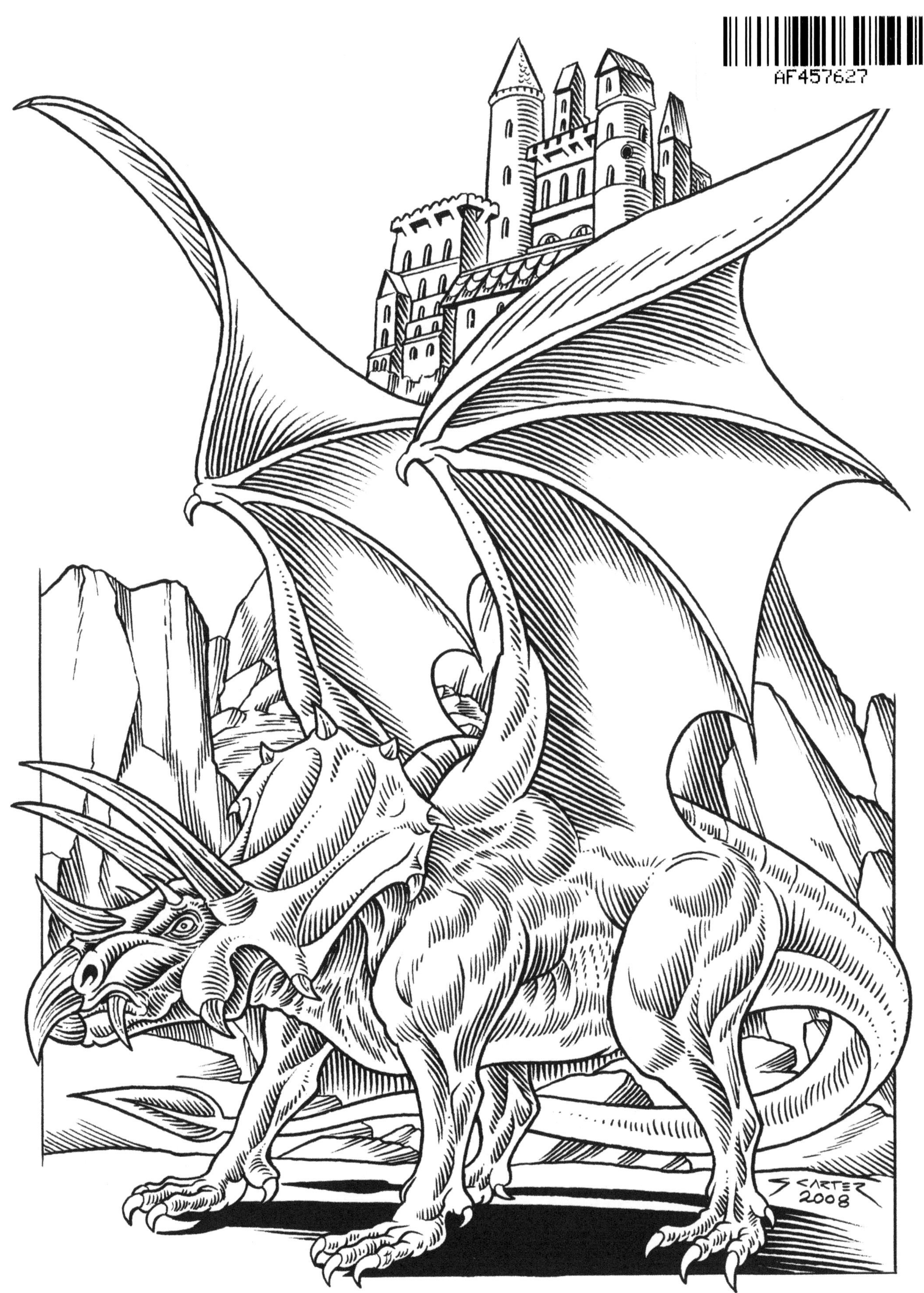

The Ceratogryph

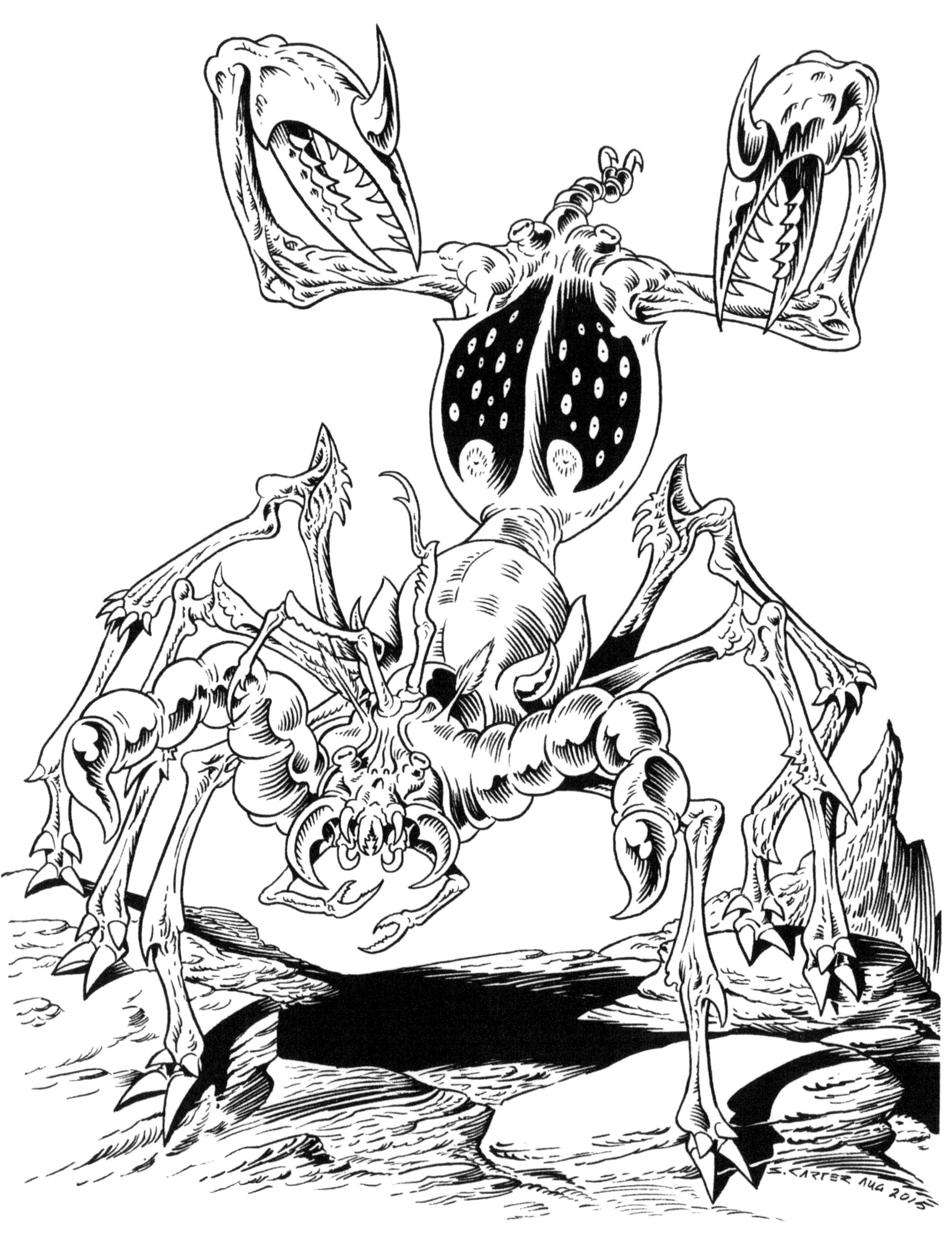

Arachnant

Illustration from "Weird Wild West 6: The Monsters of Claiborne Manor" by Carter Rydyr & Ethan Somerville

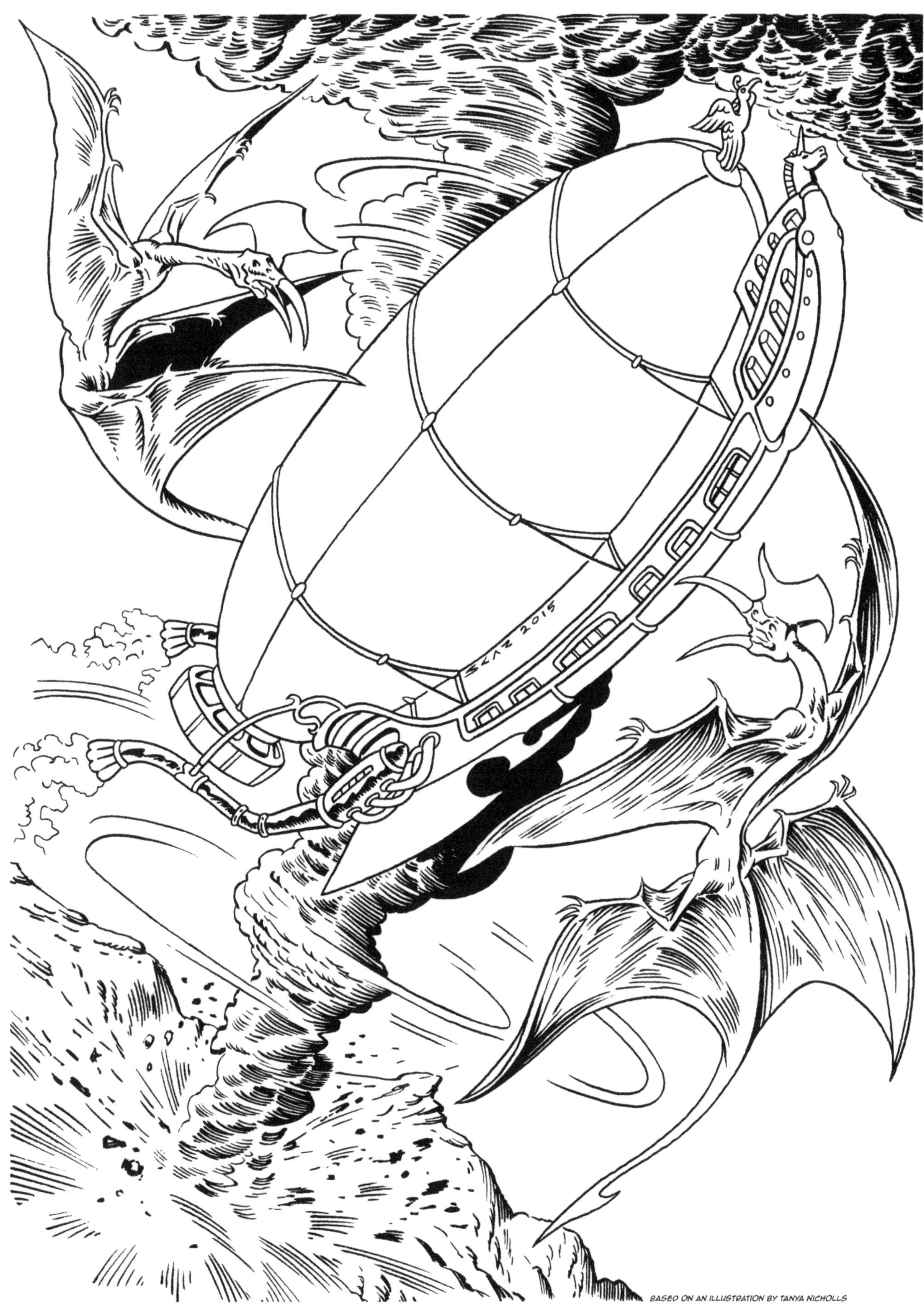

Airship in Danger

Illustration from "Weird Wild West 2: The Good, The Bad and The Zombie"
by Carter Rydyr & Ethan Somerville

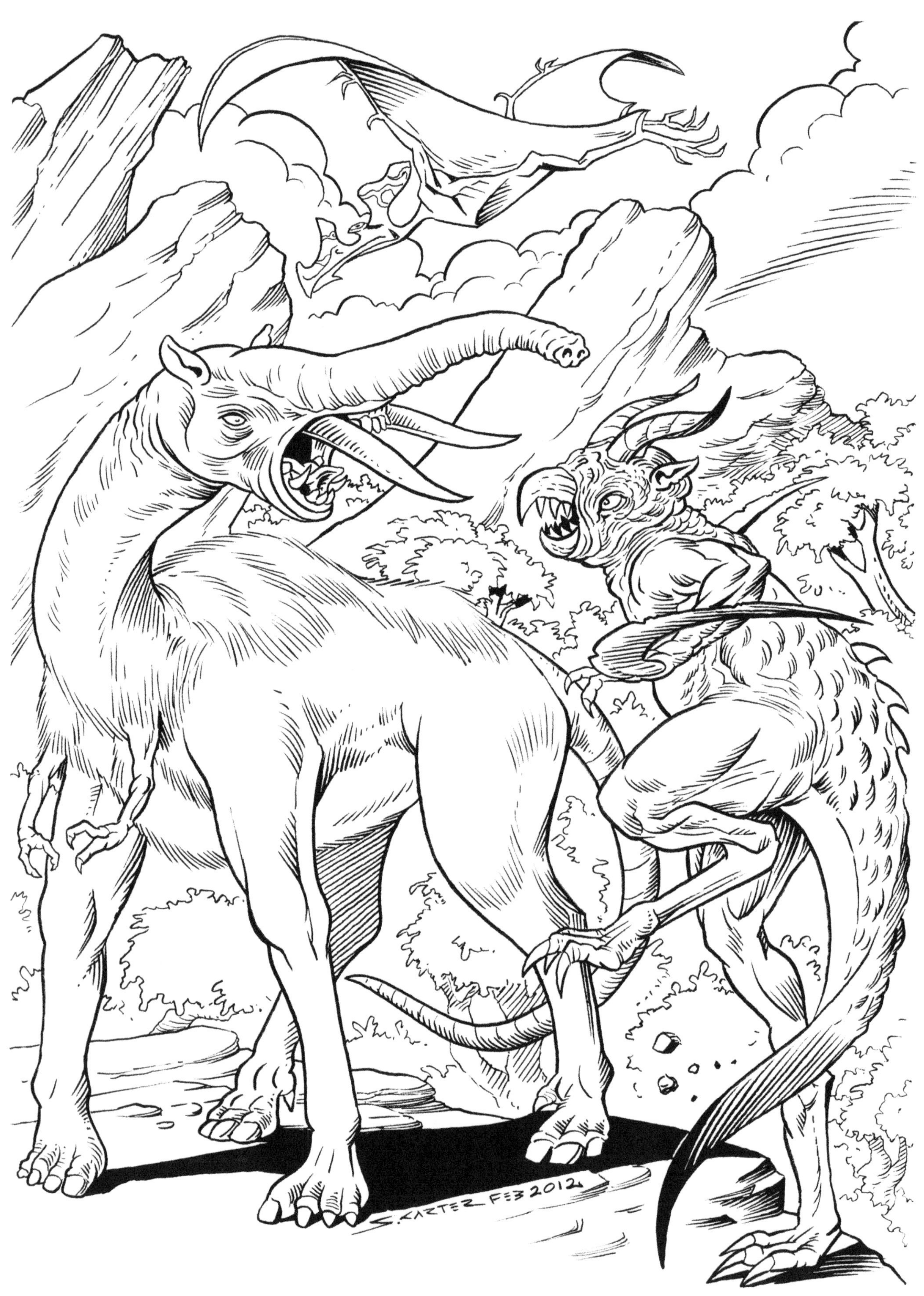

Basilisk versus Pachyderm
Illustration from "Alien Eden"

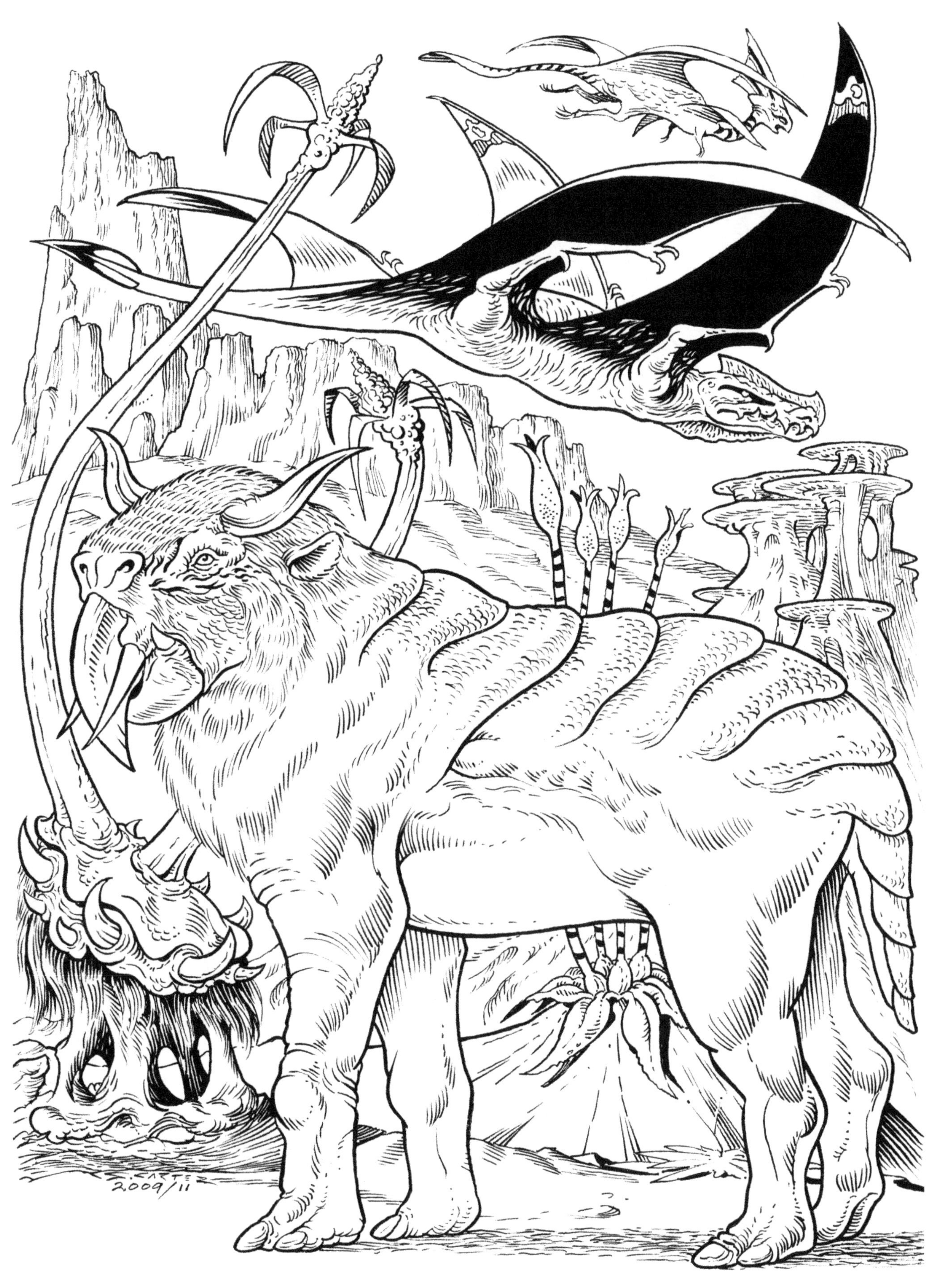

Megafauna of Nemesis
Illustration from "Alien Eden"

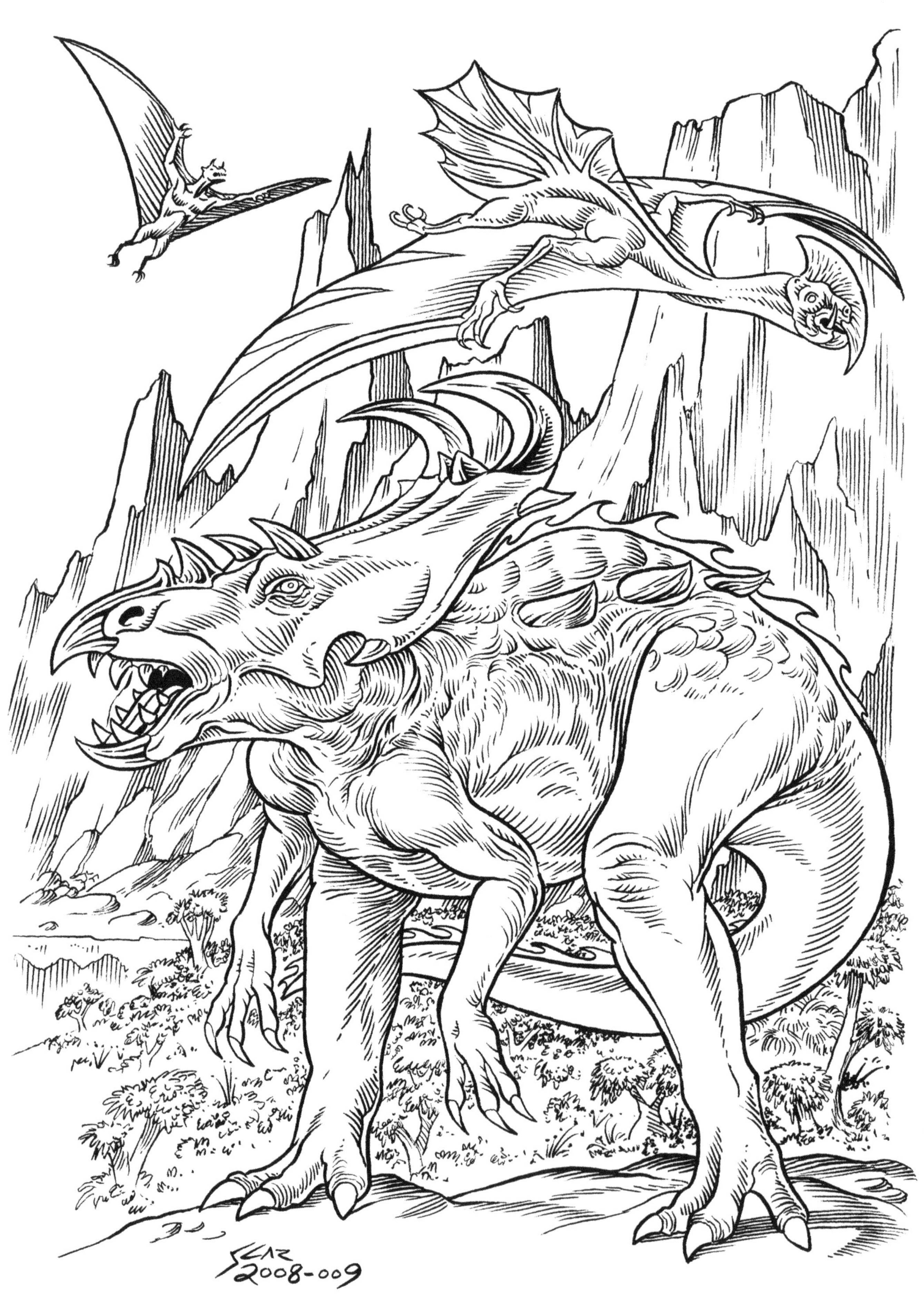

A variation of the Bipedal Carnoceratops
Illustration from "Alien Eden"

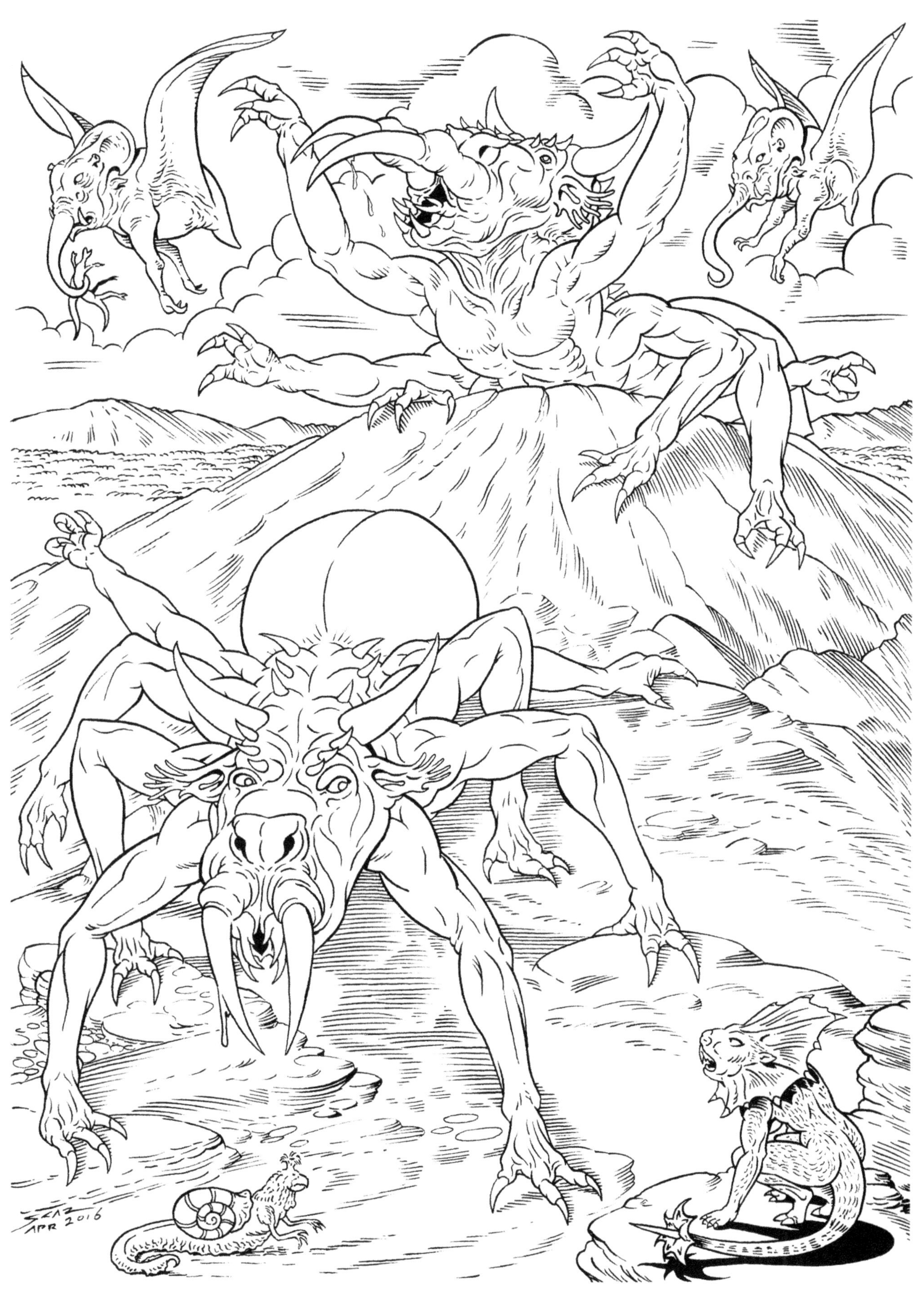

Nest of Bullarachnids

Illustration from "Weird Wild West 8: Goat Goddess of the Goldrush" by Carter Rydyr & Ethan Somerville

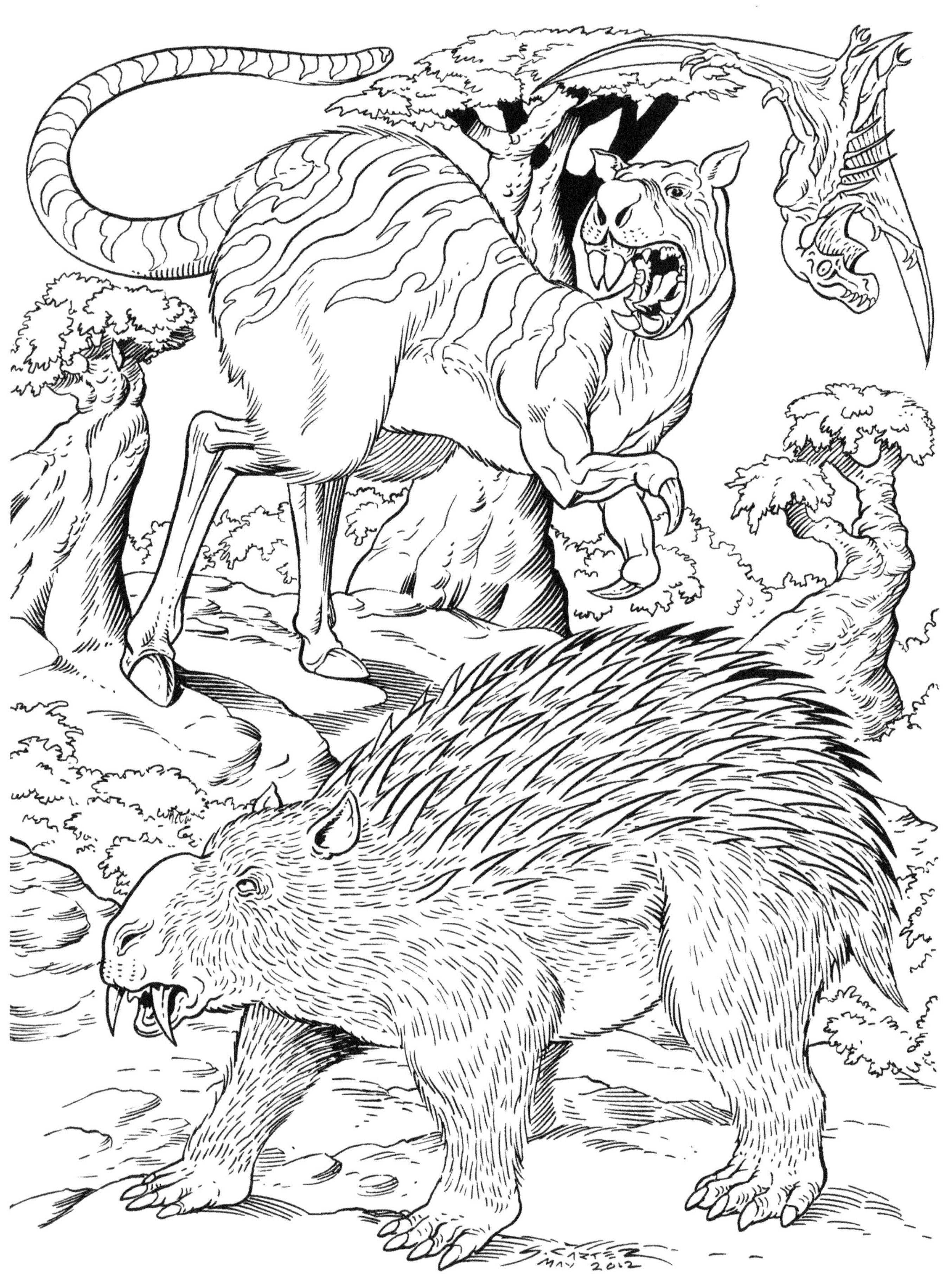

Carnivoroo and Spiny Diprotodon

Illustration from "Once Upon A Time in Australia 2 - Before the Dreamtime"

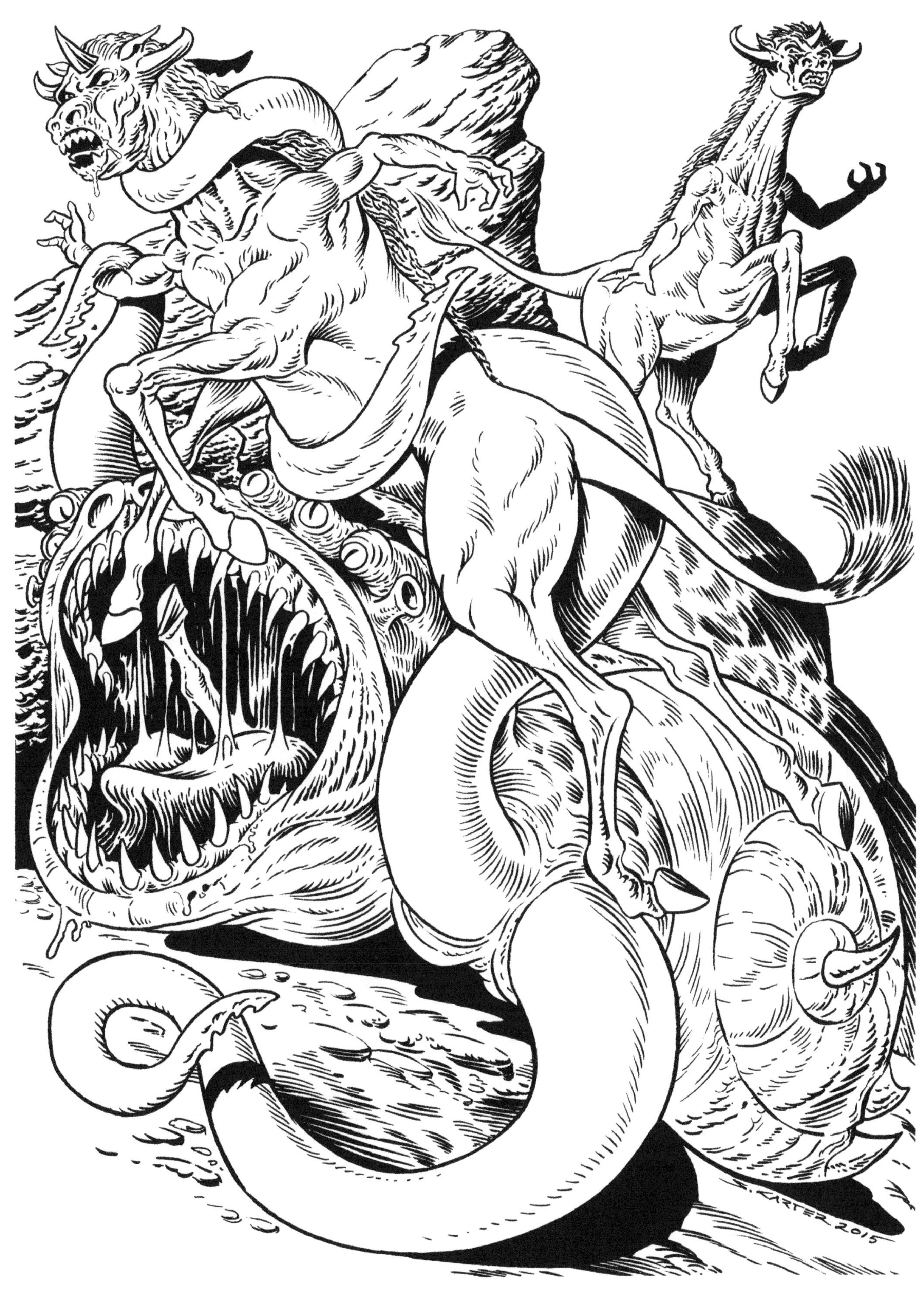

Carnivorous Snailsquid
Illustration from "Alien Eden"

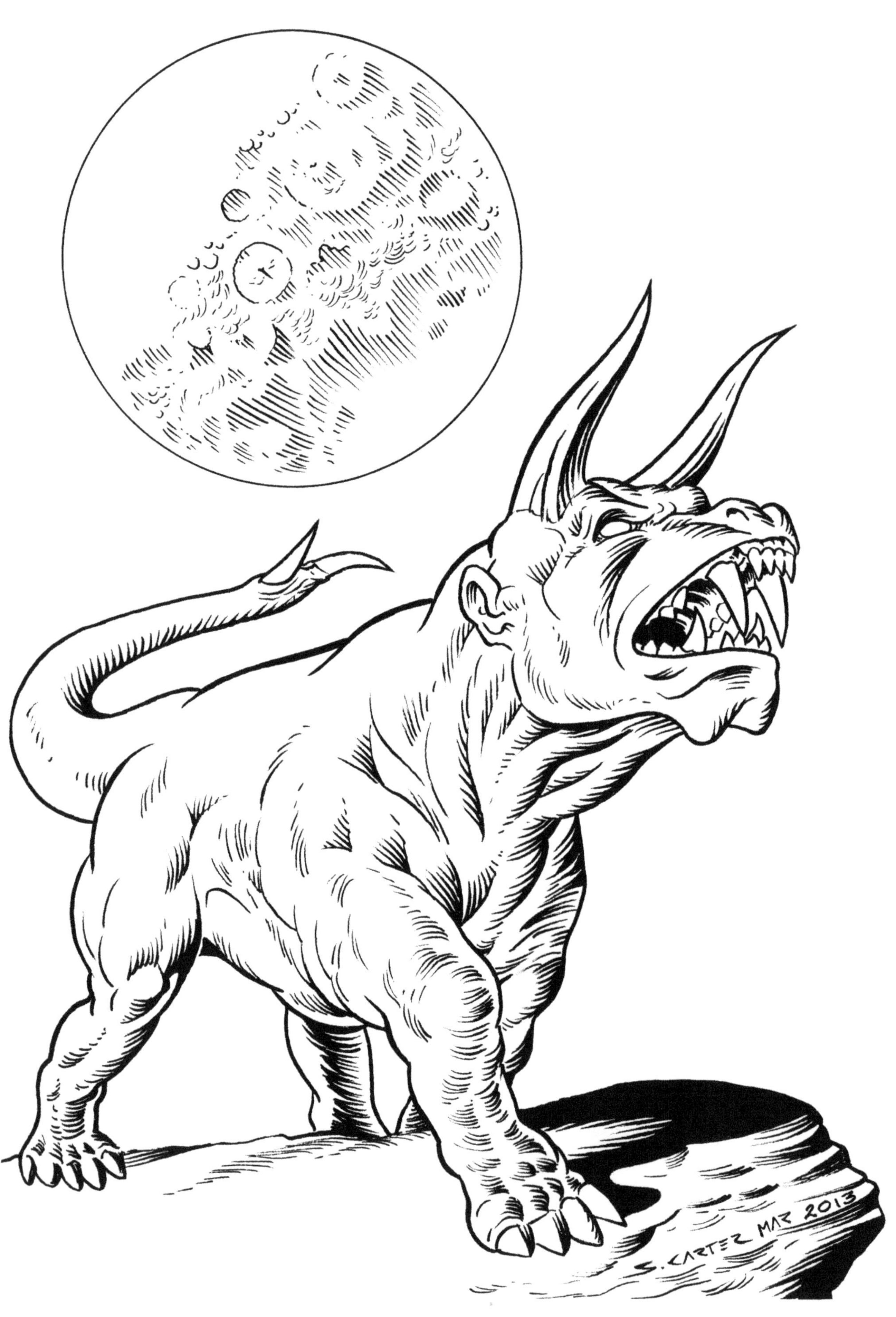

Moon of the Dagger Tusked Hurgulon
Illustration from "Alien Eden"

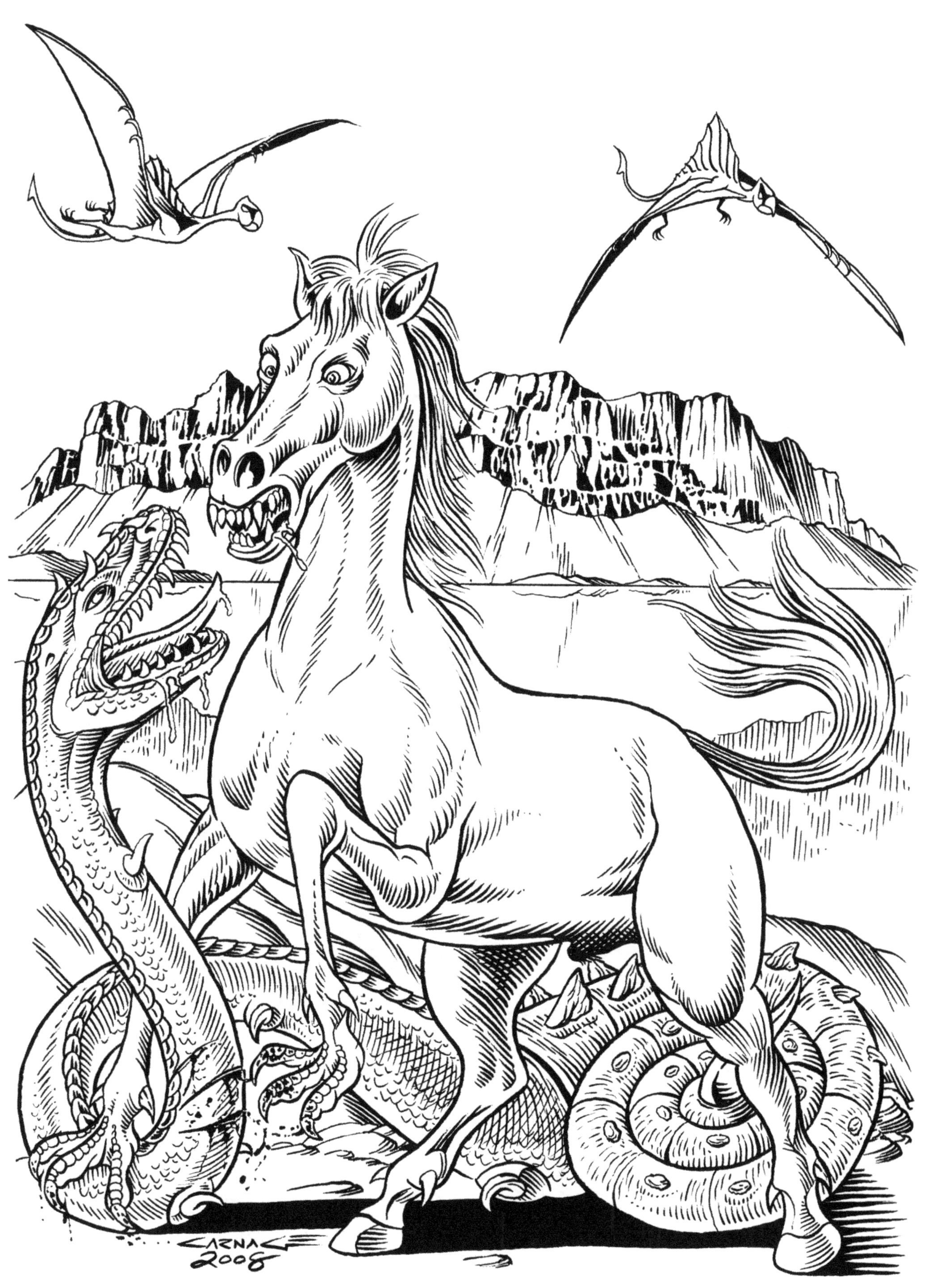

Deadly Duel of the Carnovorse and the Dragon Snail
Illustration from "Unworld - The World Before the Flood"

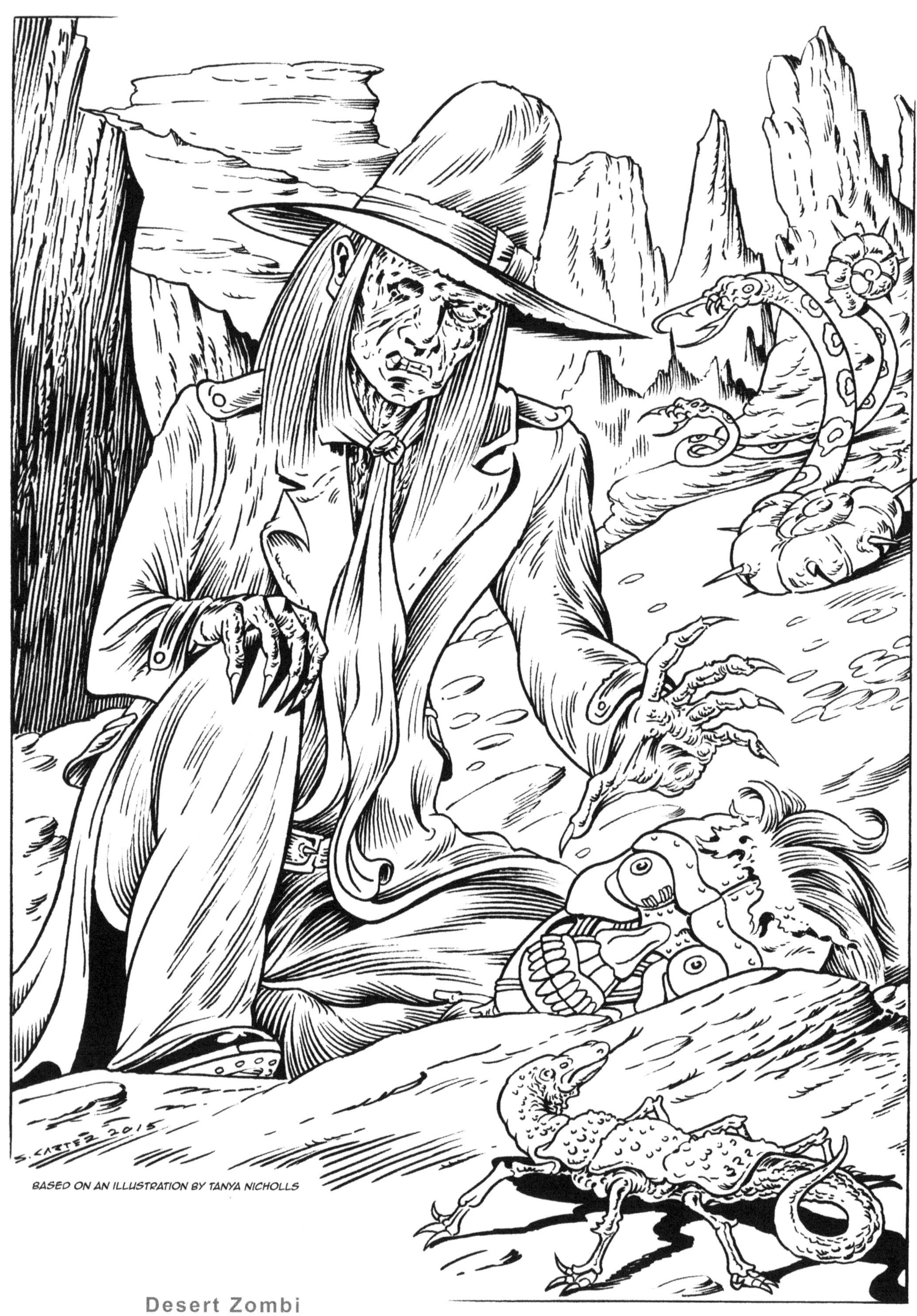

Desert Zombi

Illustration from "Weird Wild West 1: Hell Dorado"
by Carter Rydyr & Ethan Somerville

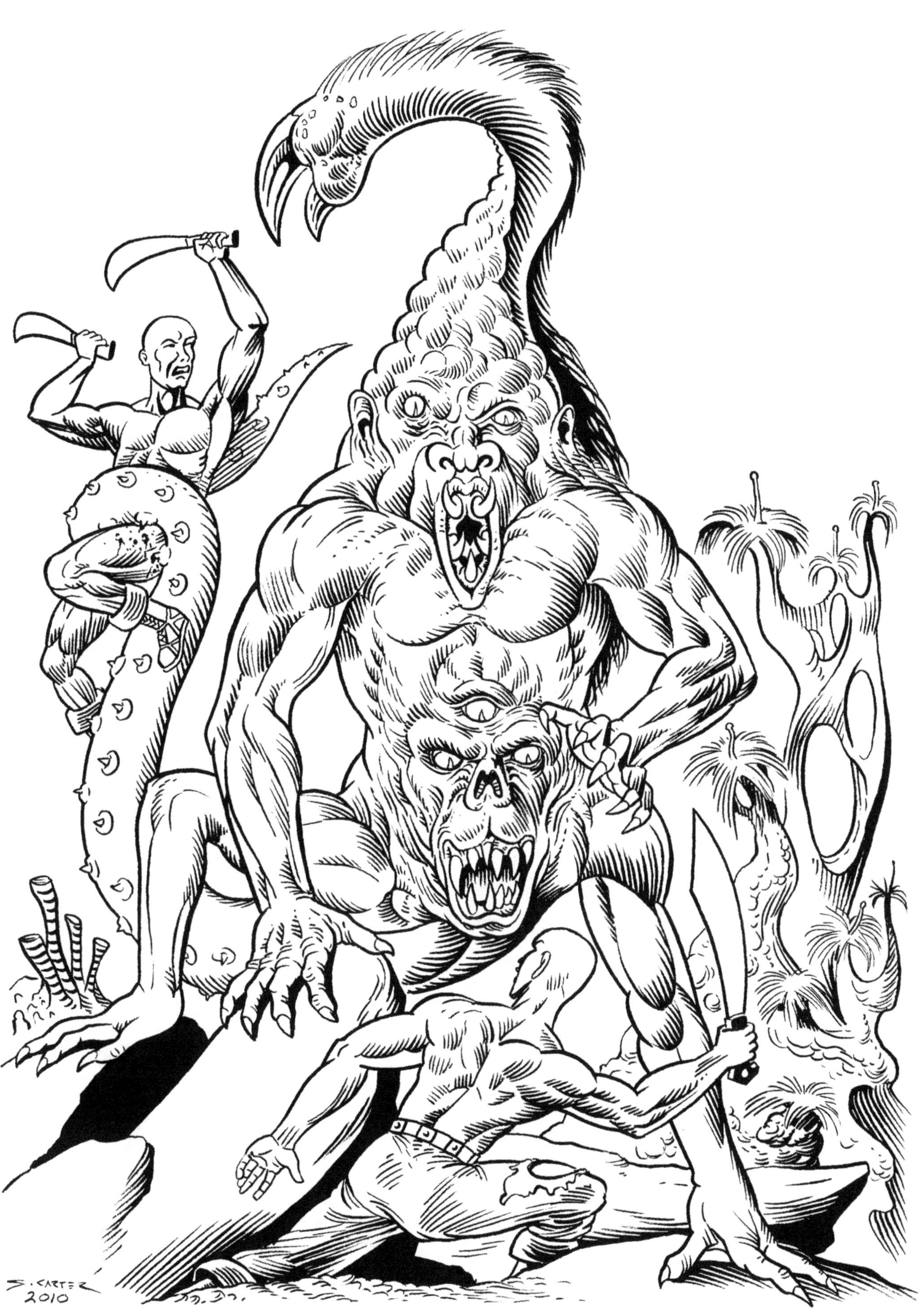

Misshapen Hybrid of Hybridos

Illustration from "Hybridos - The Lost Planet"

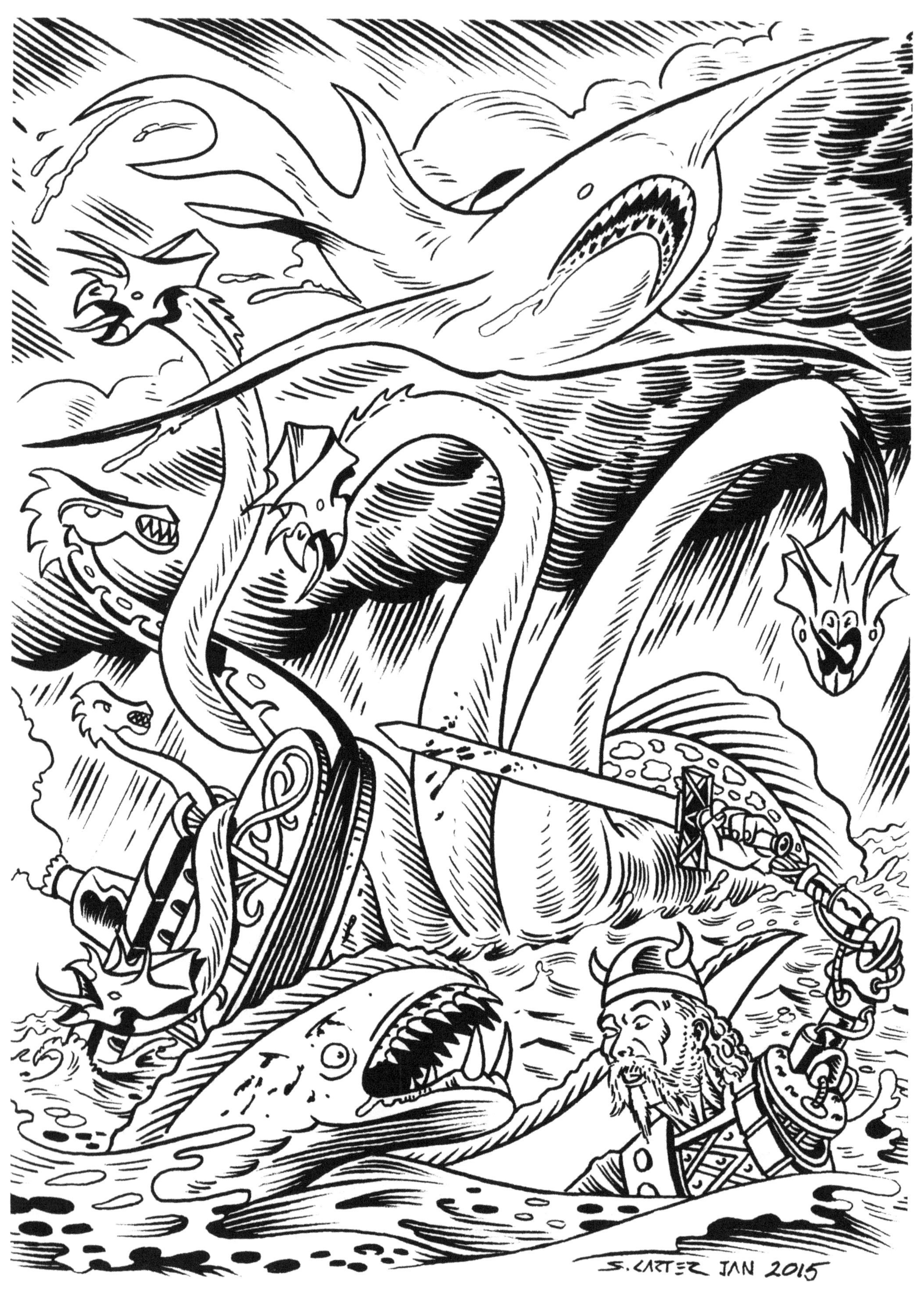

Harbour of Doom

Illustration from "Weird Wild West 4: The Vyking War"

by Carter Rydyr & Ethan Somerville

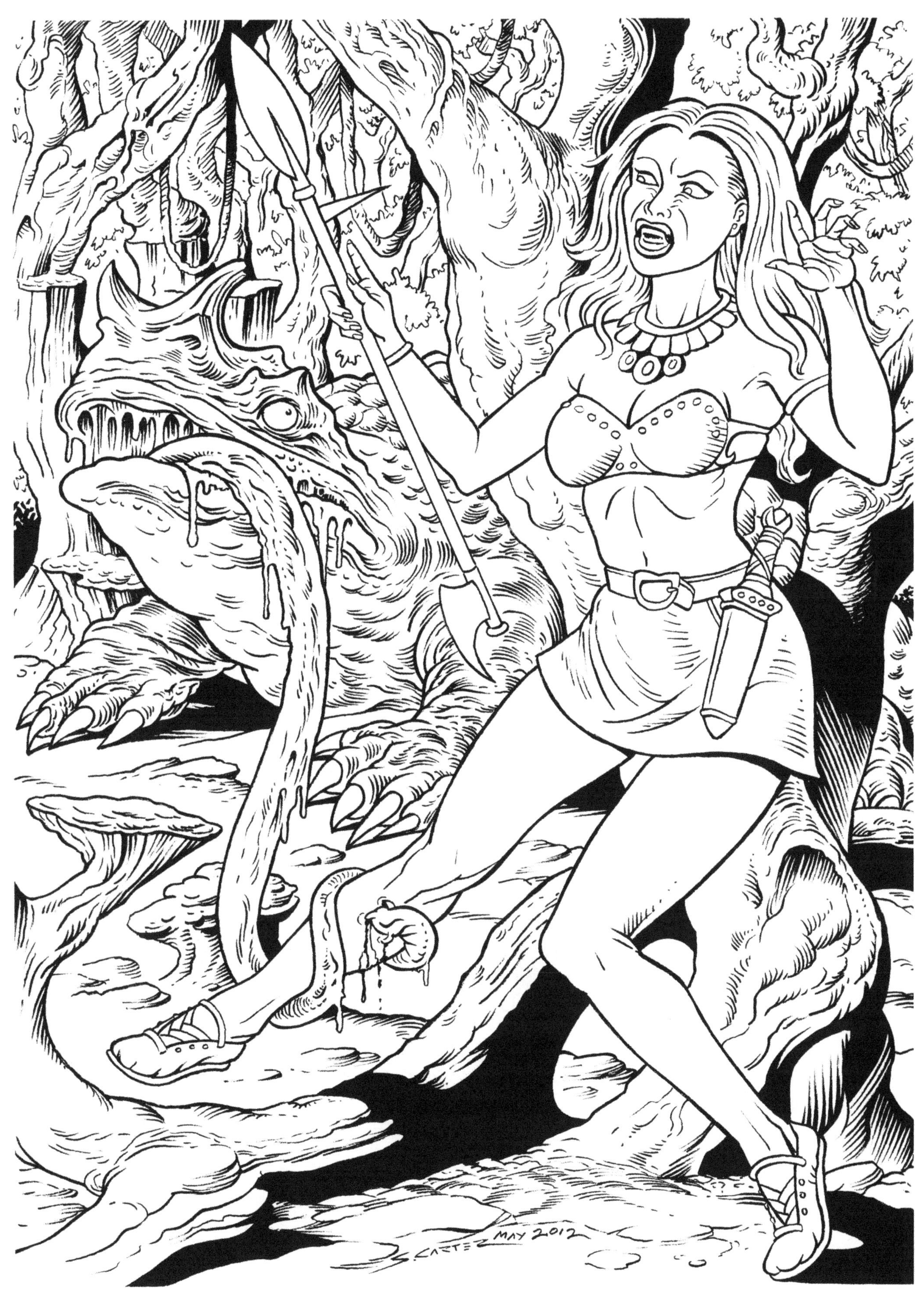

Fajessa Attacked by a Giant Batrachian

Illustration from "Once Upon A Time in Australia 3: Nocturalis"

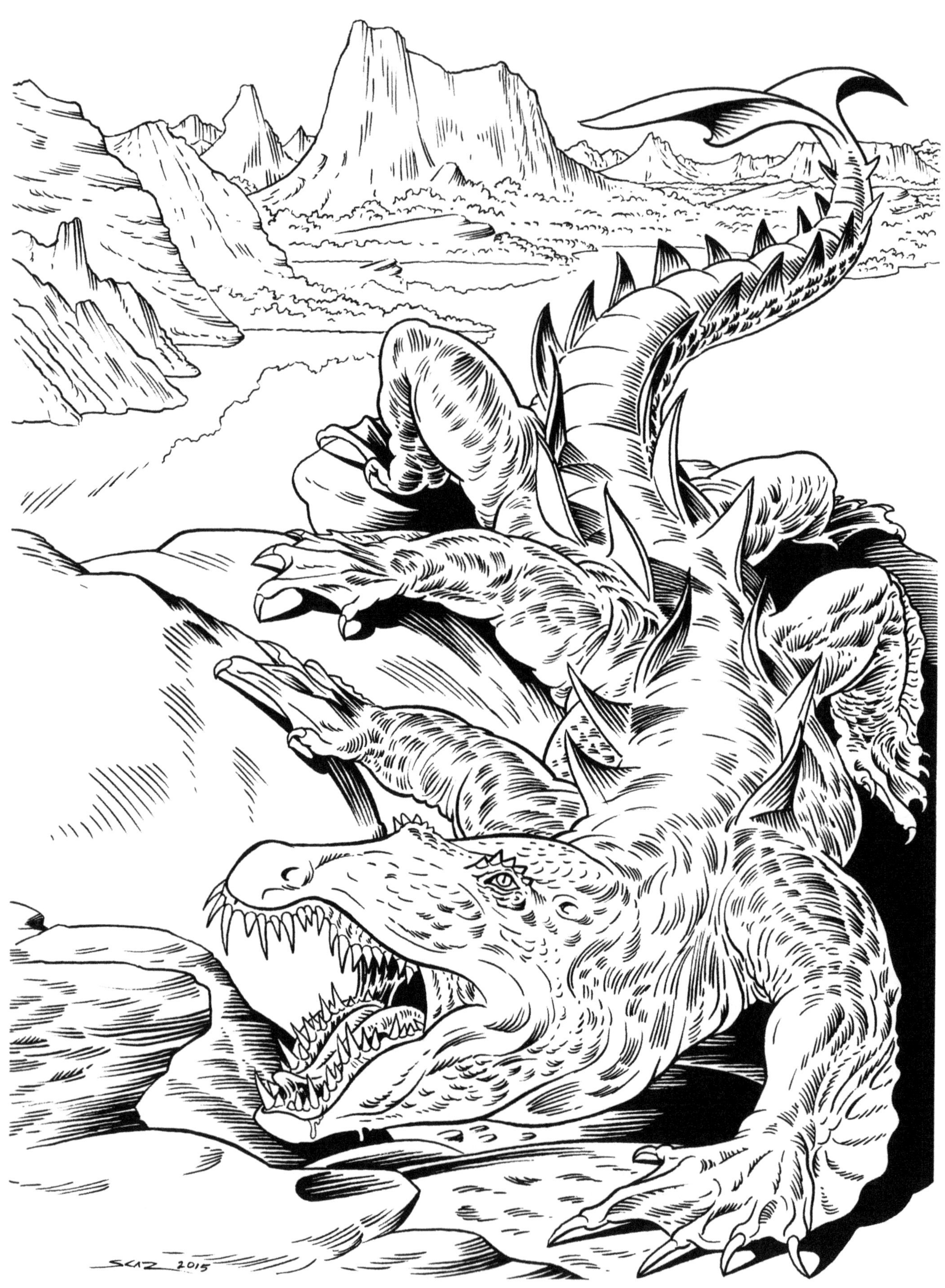

Hexasaurian

Illustration from "Weird Wild West 2: The Good, The Bad and The Zombie" by Carter Rydyr & Ethan Somerville

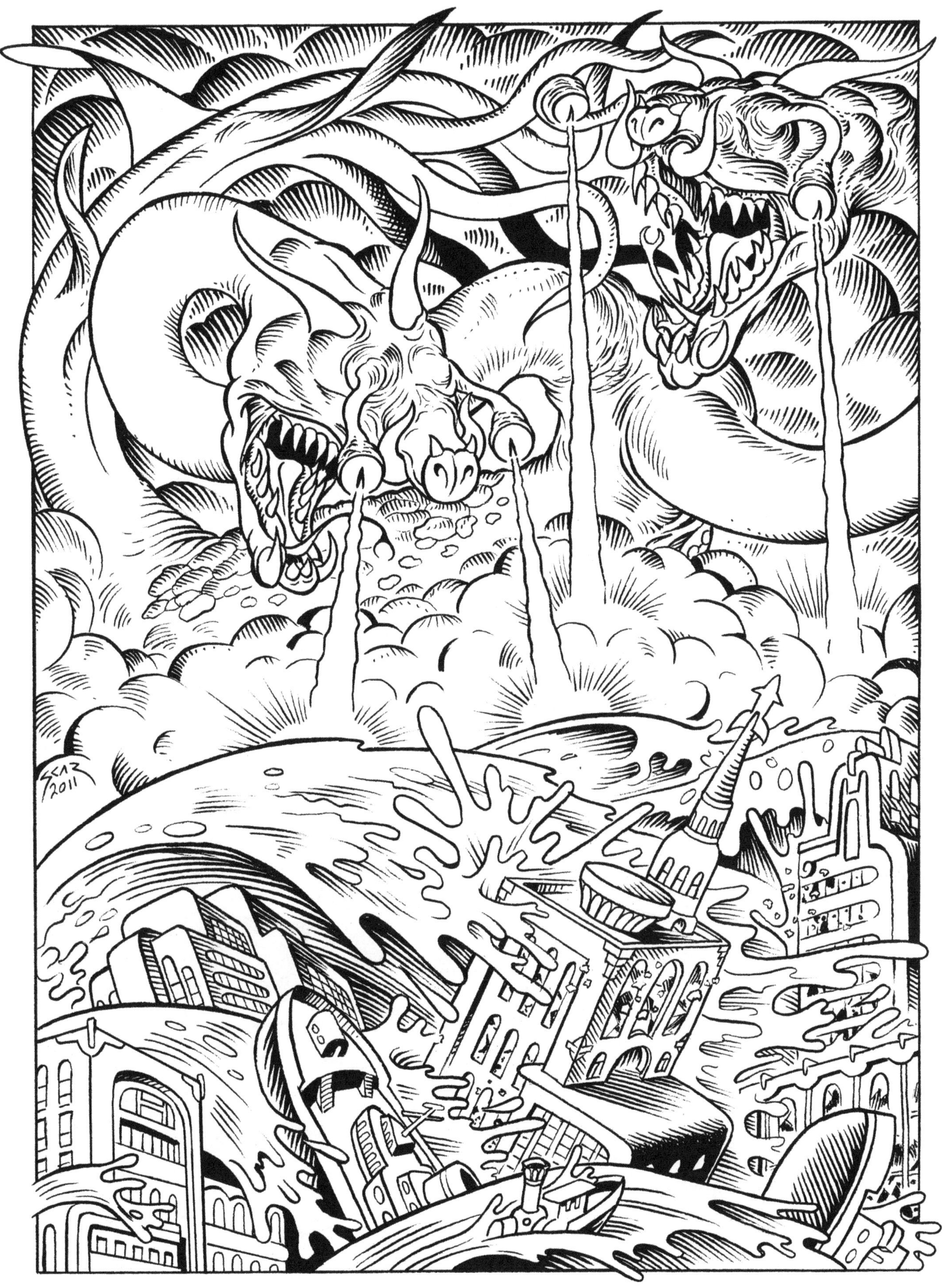

Oriental Leviathan

Illustration for "Aftershock - Artists Respond to Disaster in Japan"

Biguglyrobot Publishing

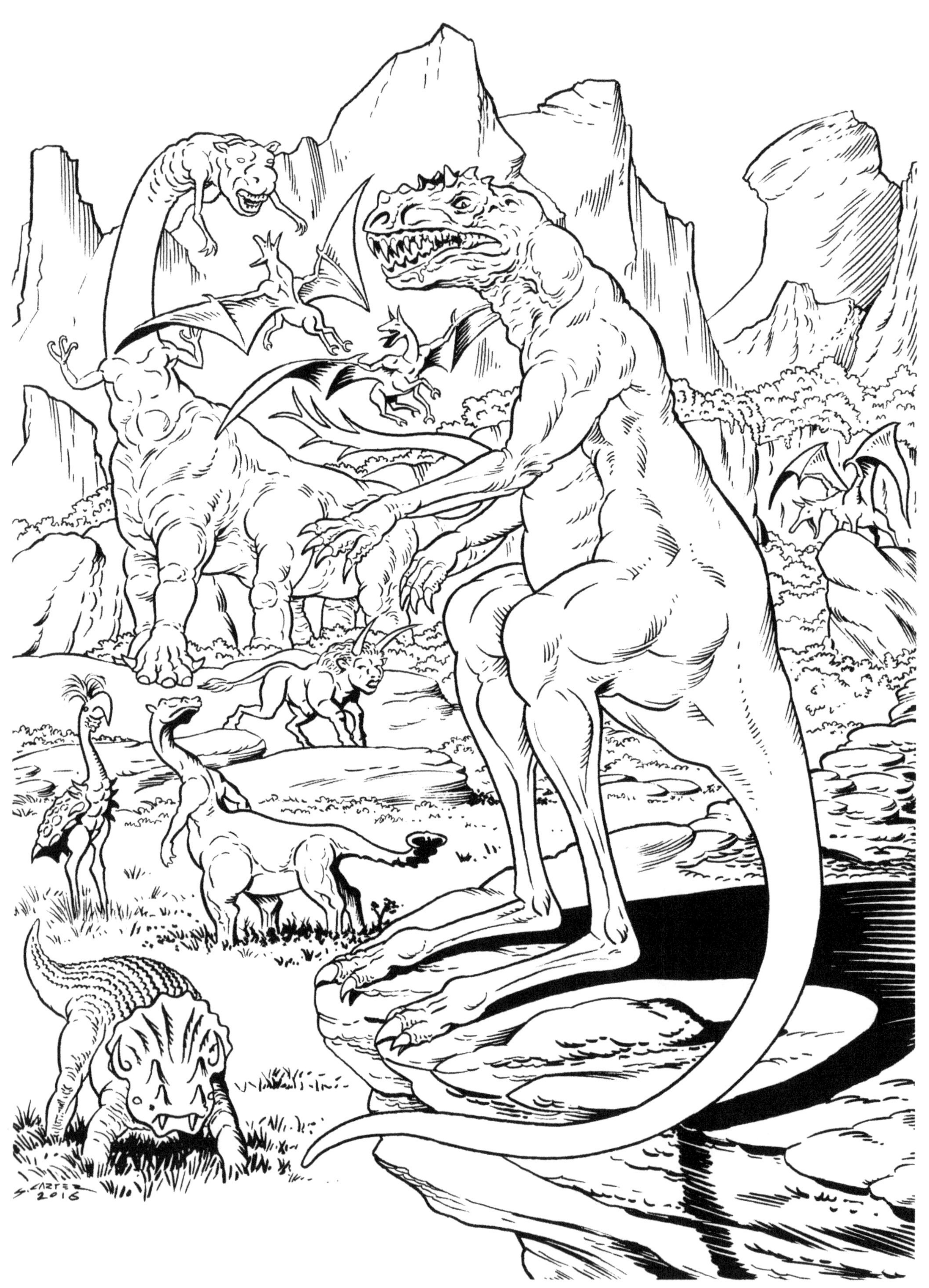

Kangasaurus

Illustration from "Once Upon A Time in Australia"

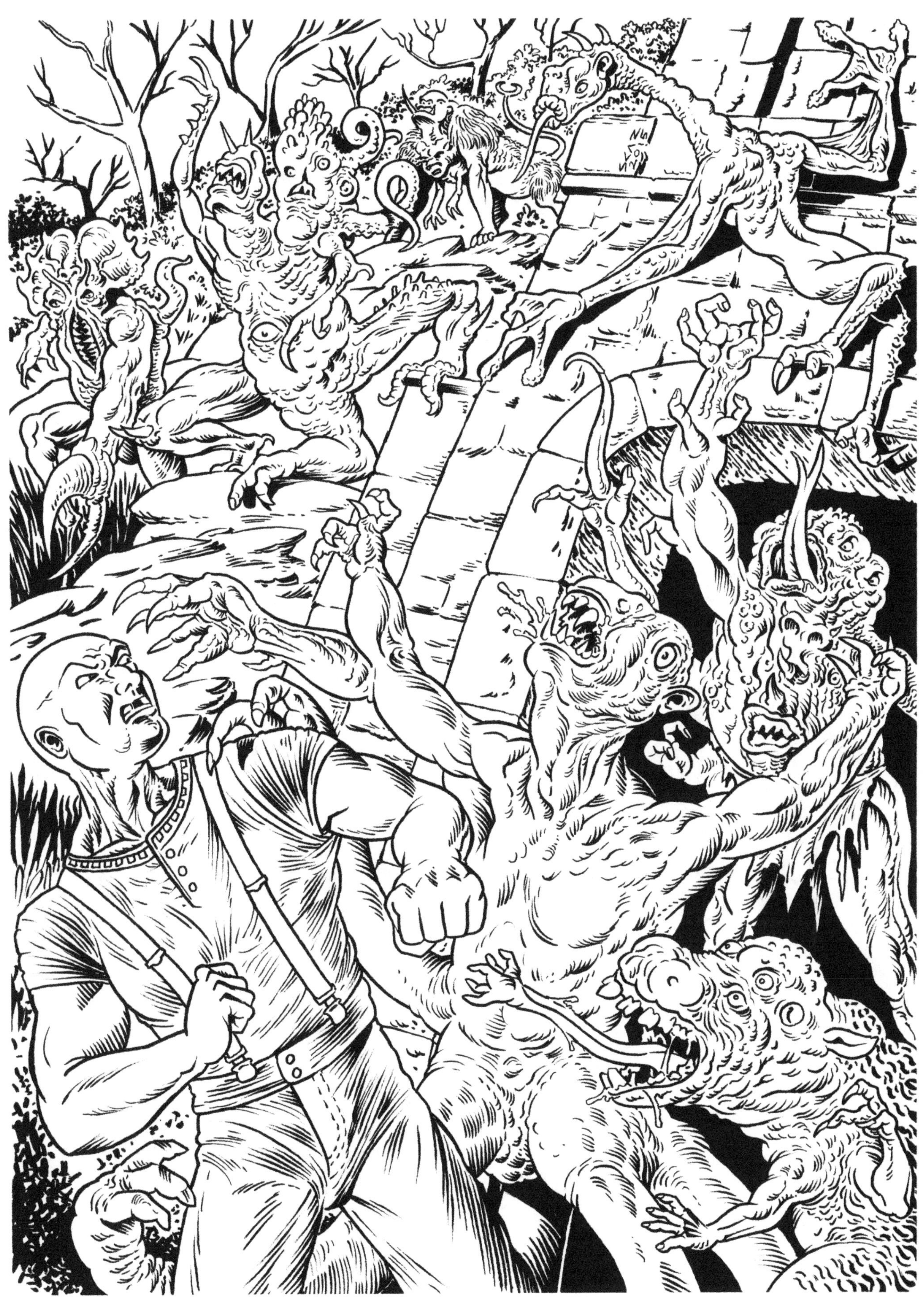

King Skin Confronts the Mutant Masses

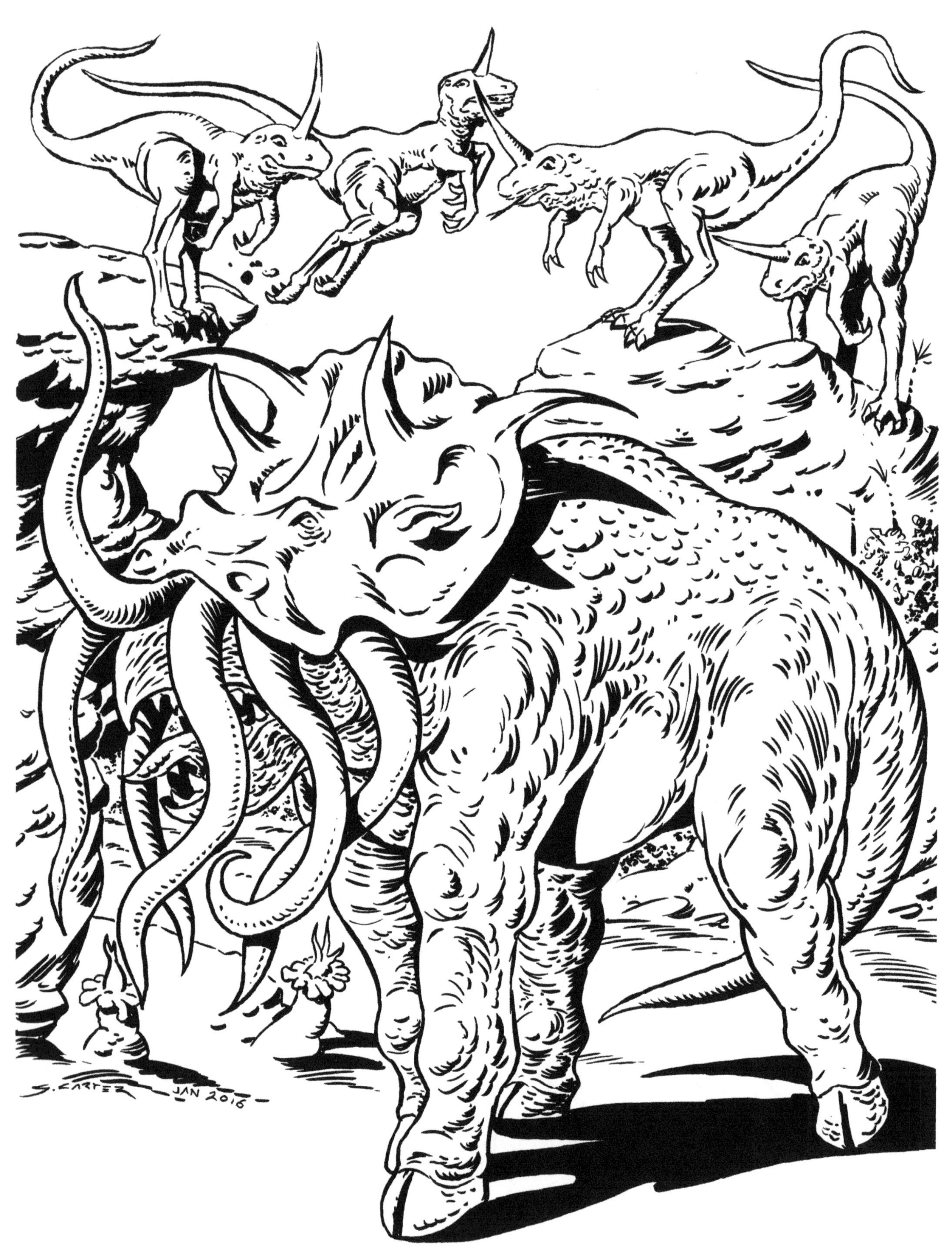

Kraken Headed Pachyderm
Illustration from "Alien Eden"

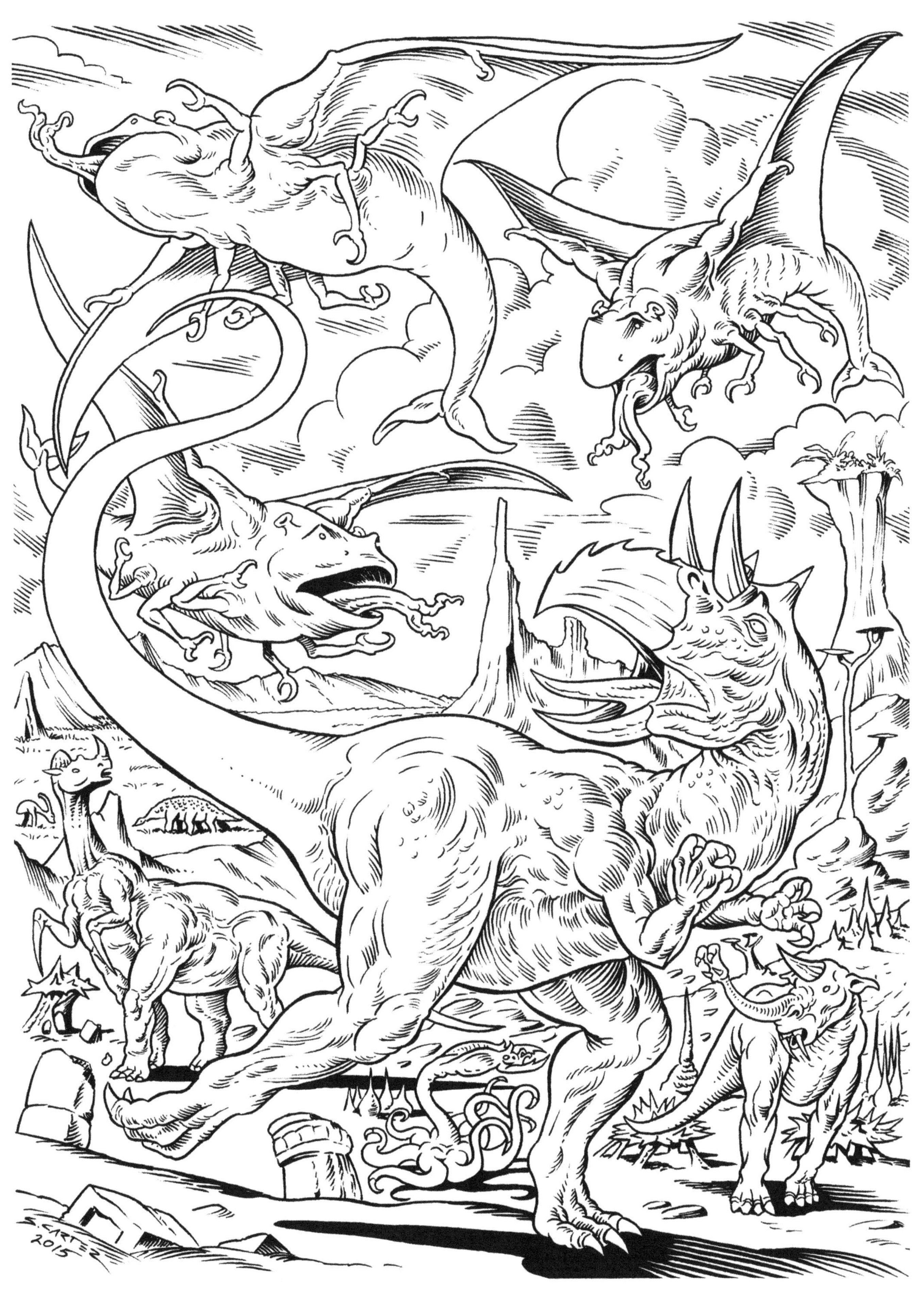

Menace of the Flying King Toadfish
Illustration from "Alien Eden"

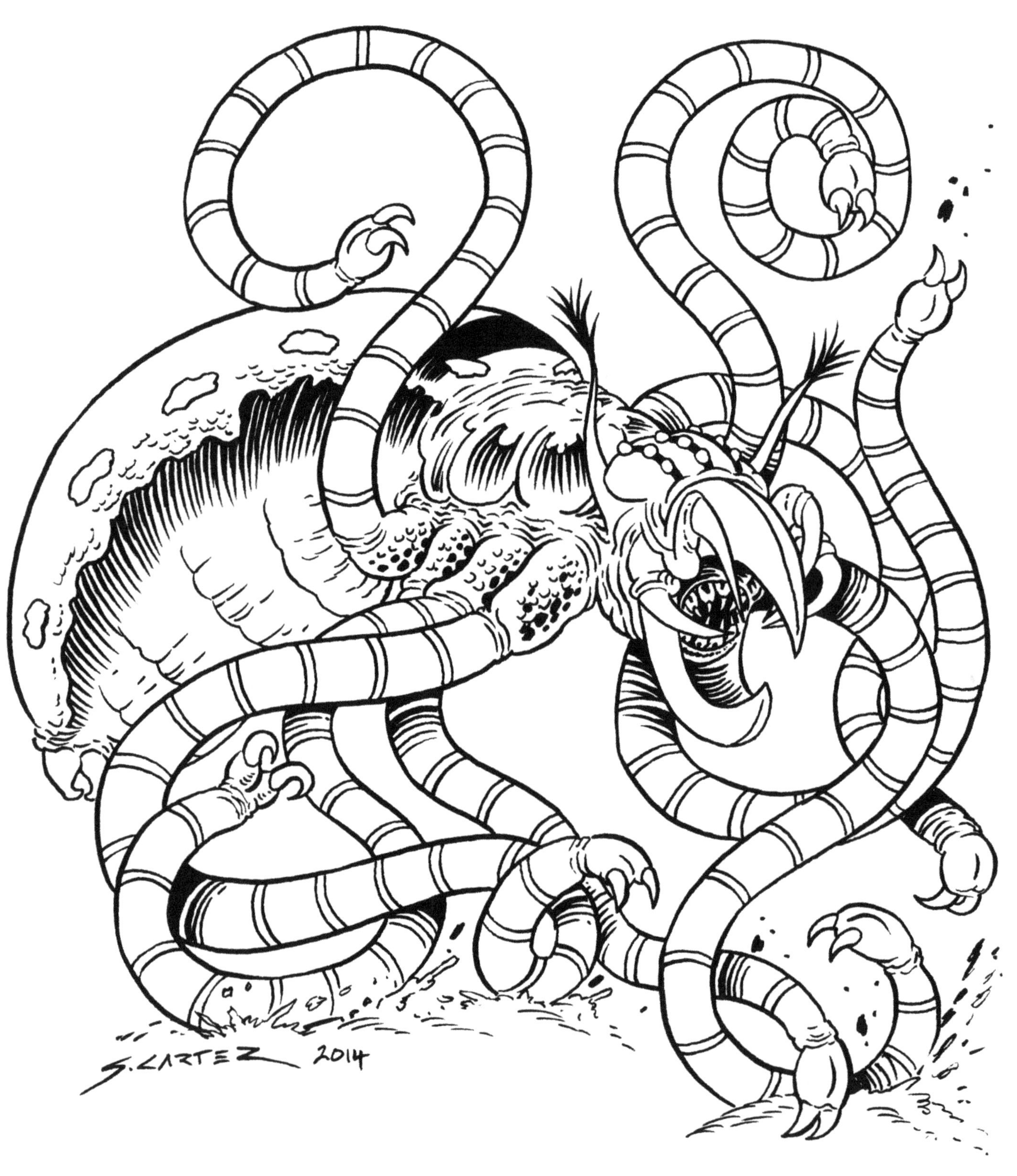

Kraken Spider

Illustration from “Weird Wild West 3: The Freaks of Mojo County”
by Carter Rydyr & Ethan Somerville

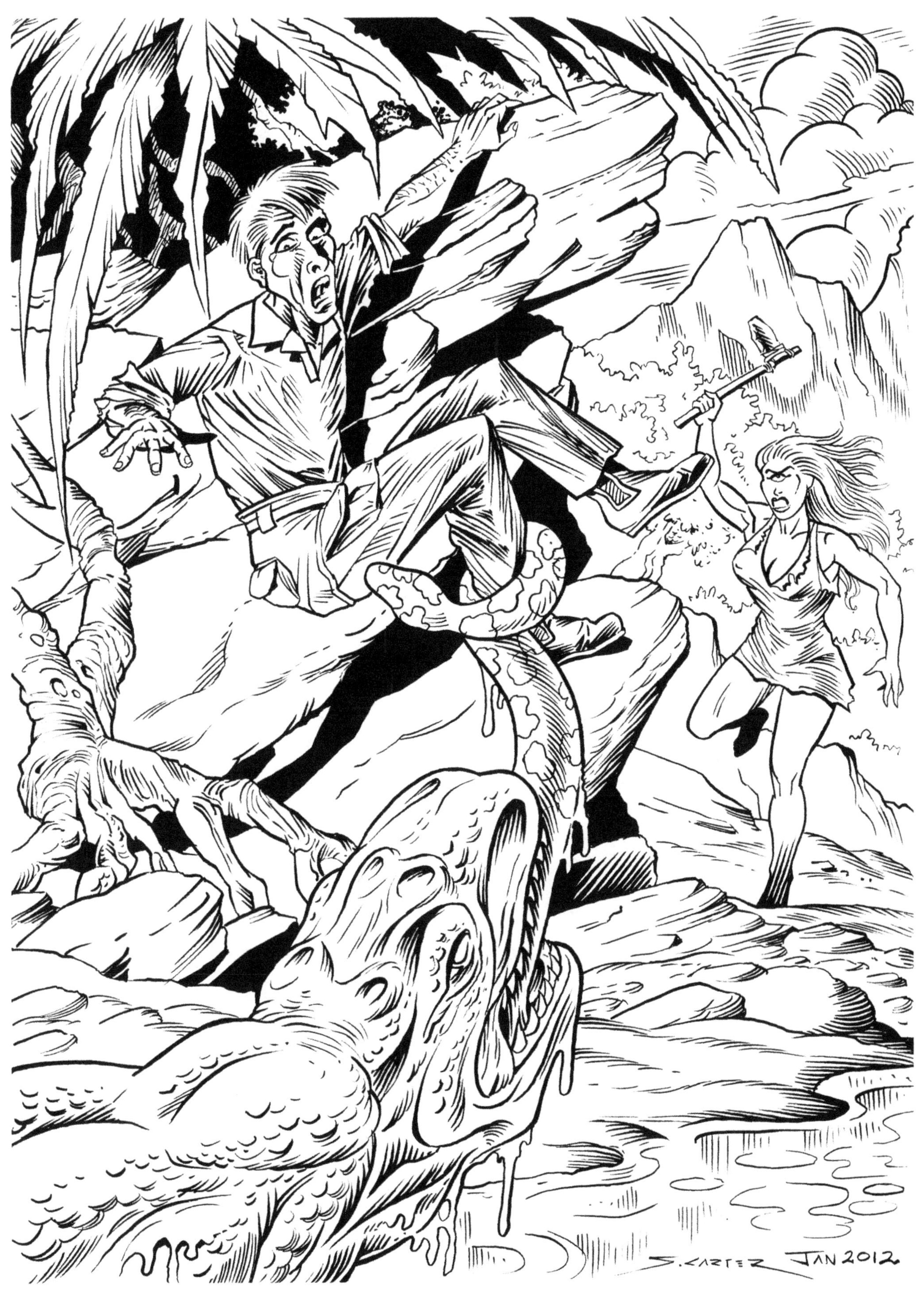

Riverside Ambush

Illustration from "Once Upon A Time in Australia 2 - Before the Dreamtime"

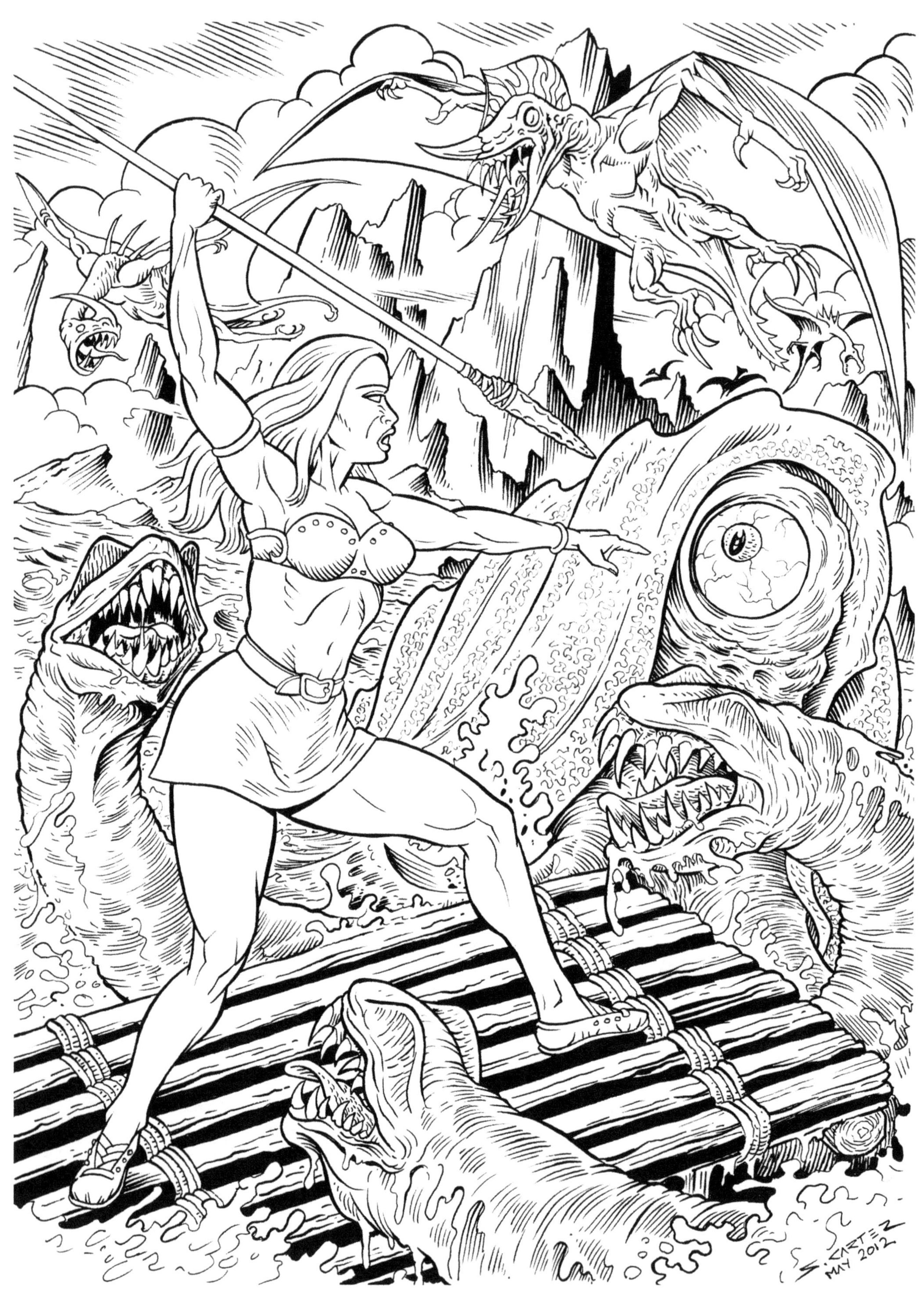

Fajessa fends off a Kraken

Illustration from "Once Upon A Time in Australia 3: Nocturalis"

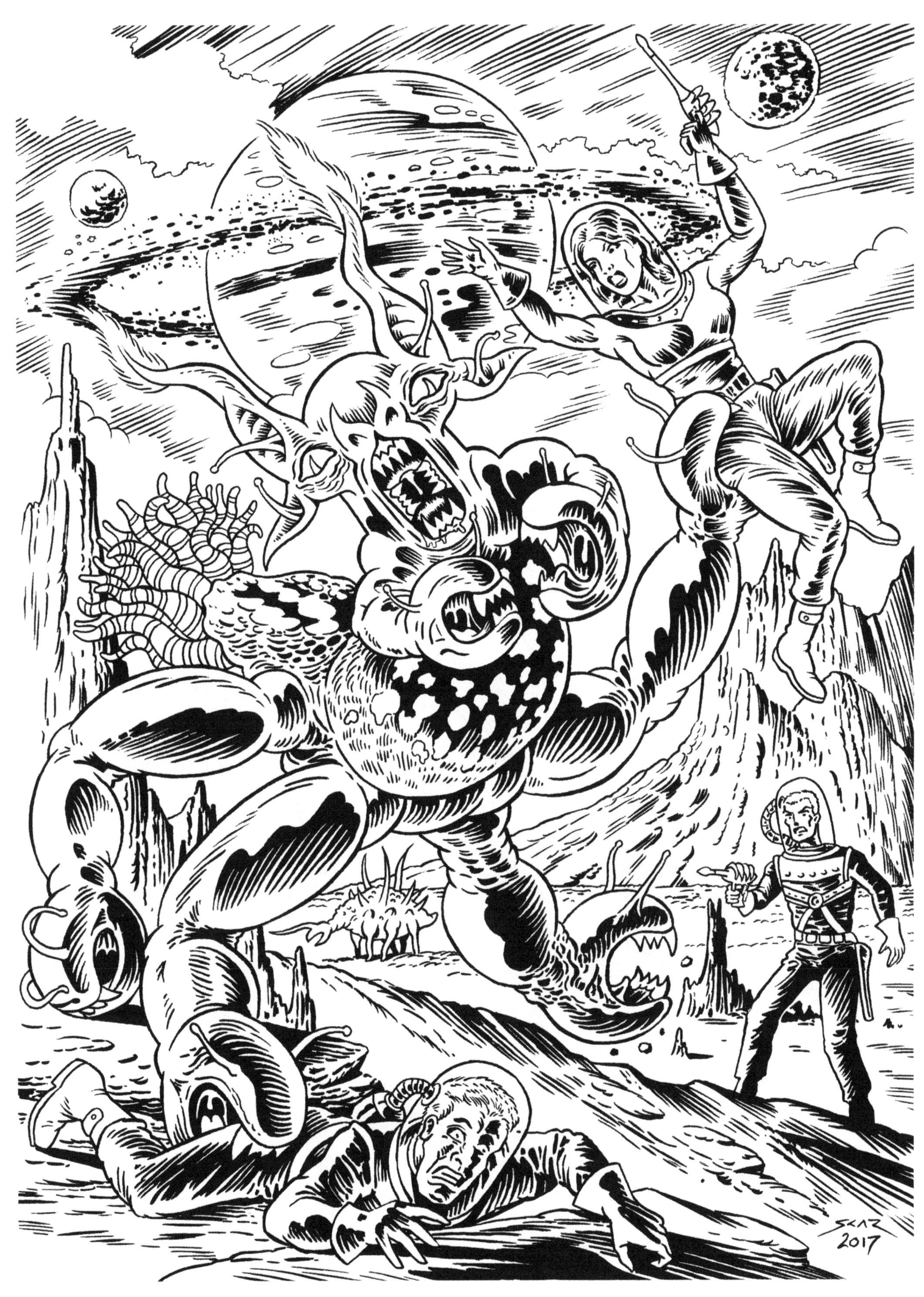

Menace of the Astro-Storm Planet

Homage to the Atlas Era Monster Comics

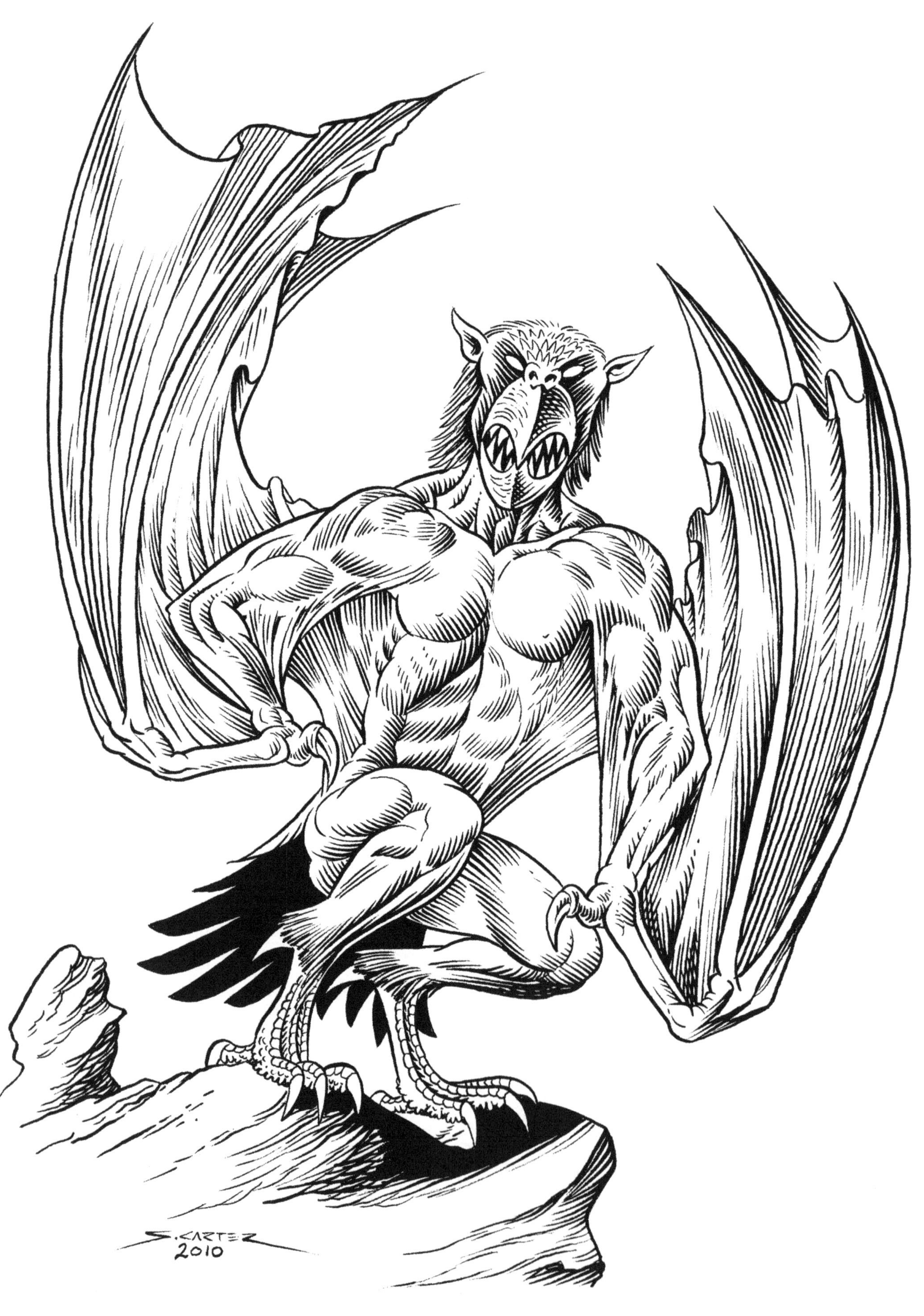

Predatory Terror Beaked Pterobat
Illustration from "Alien Eden"

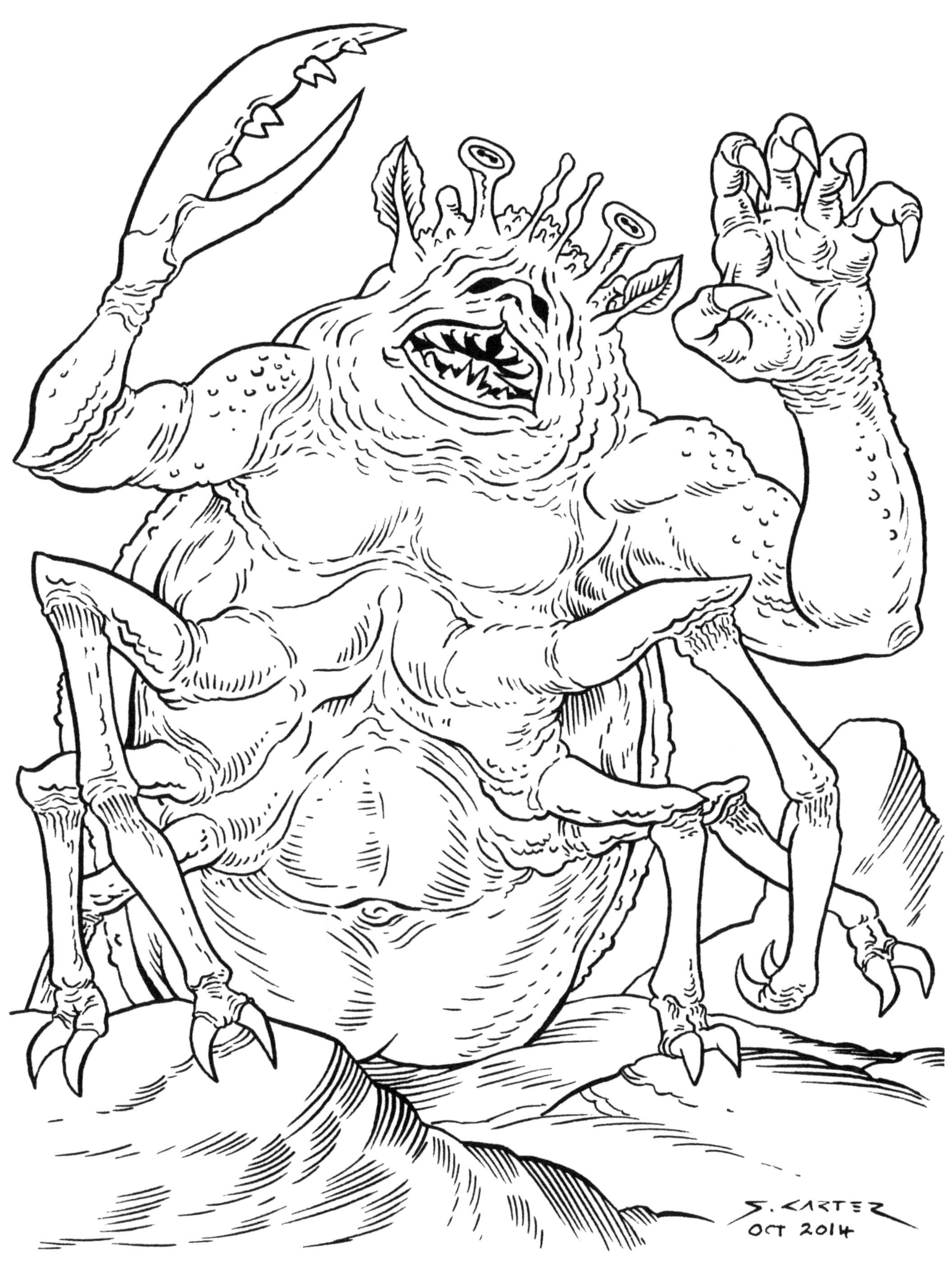

Monstrous Mung Mutant
Illustration from "Weird Wild West 7: The Creatures From Hacking River"
by Carter Rydyr & Ethan Somerville

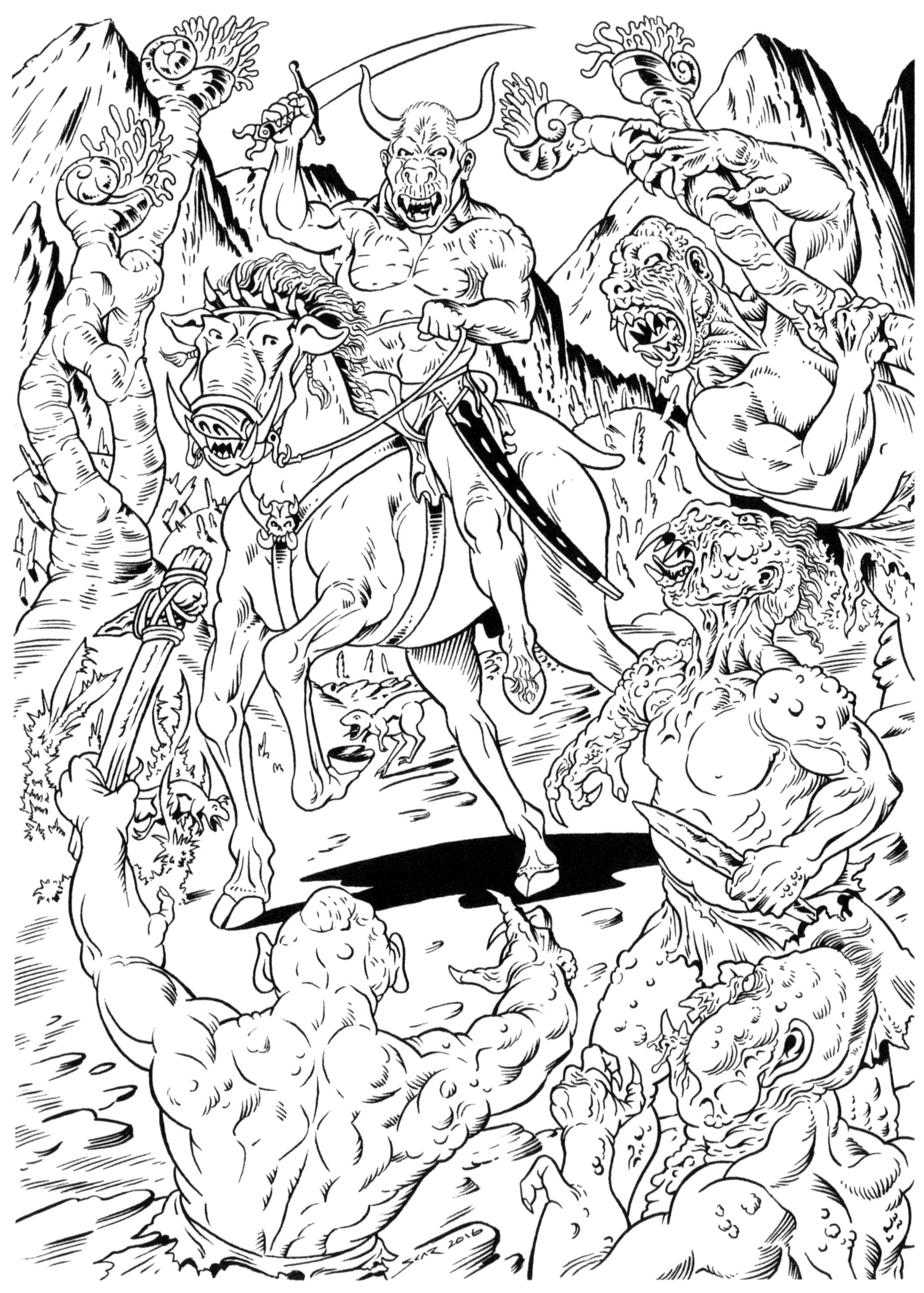

Mung Trolls Attack

Illustration from "Six-Gun Cindy - Menace of the Mung Trolls"

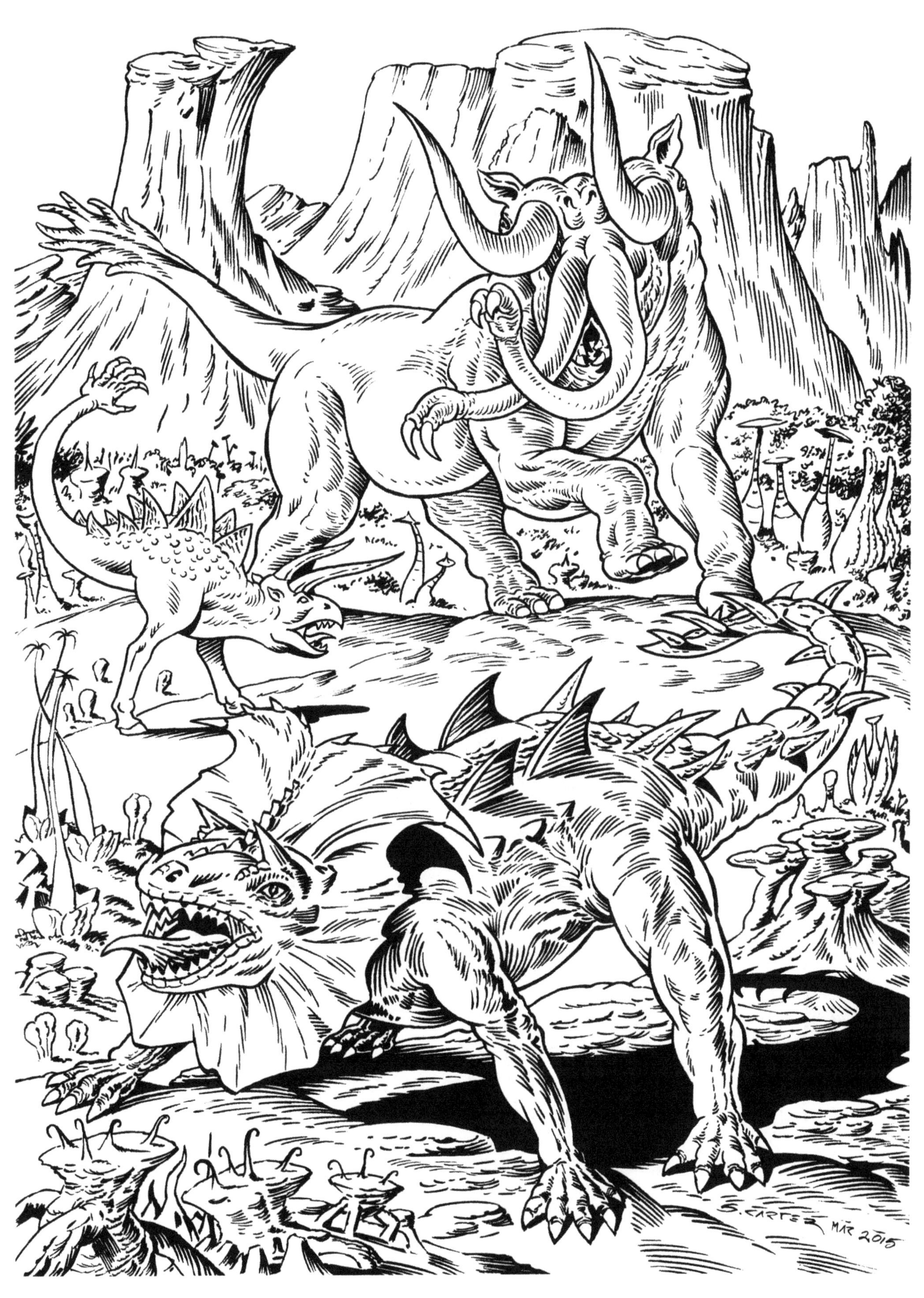

Nemesean Fauna
Illustration from "Alien Eden"

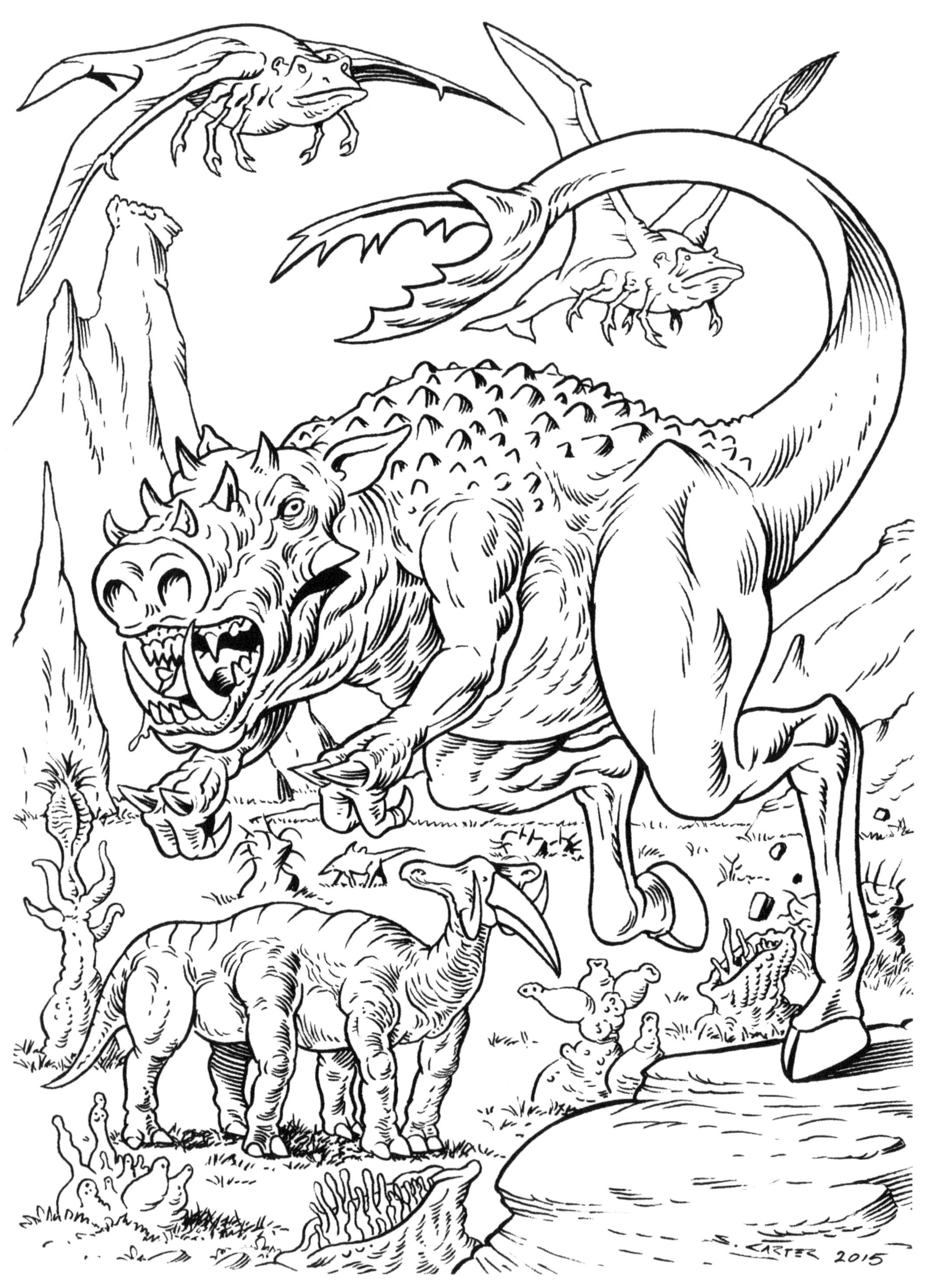

Nipper-Tailed Sauroboar

Illustration from "Alien Eden"

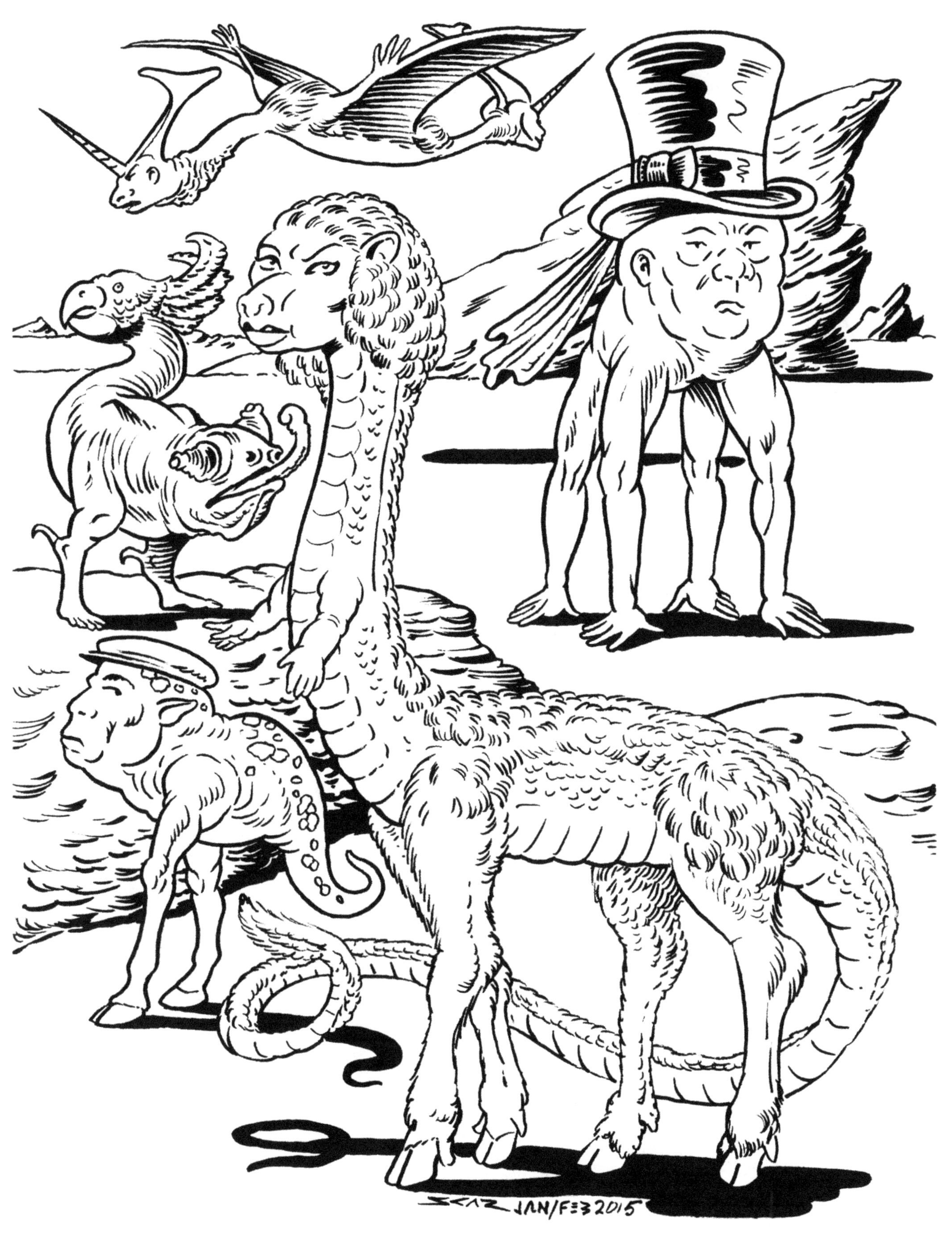

Obscure Misfits of the Way Out West

Illustration from "Weird Wild West 5: Deja Voodoo"

by Carter Rydyr & Ethan Somerville

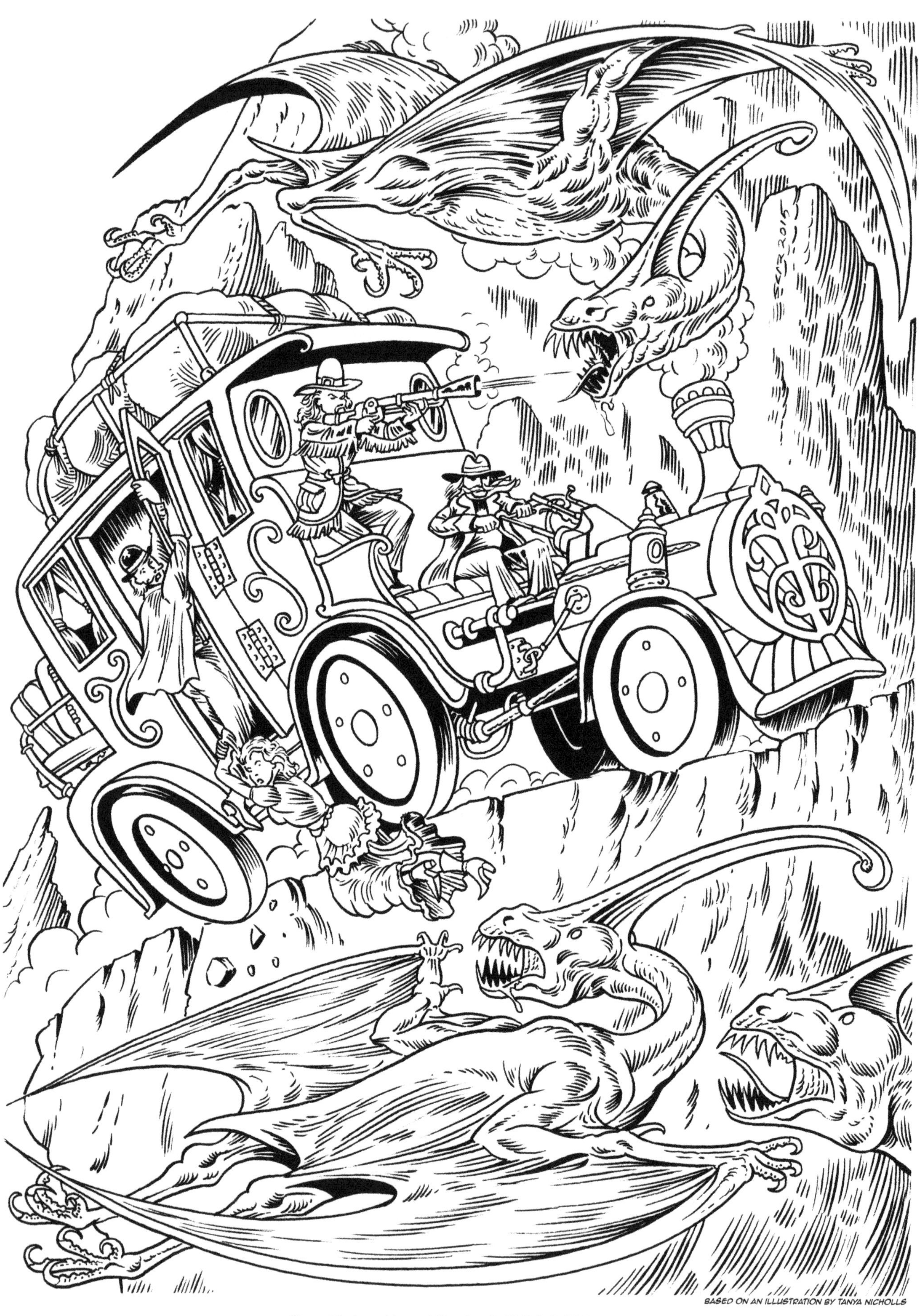

Peril in the Weird Wild West
Illustration from "Weird Wild West 1: Hell Dorado"
by Carter Rydyr & Ethan Somerville

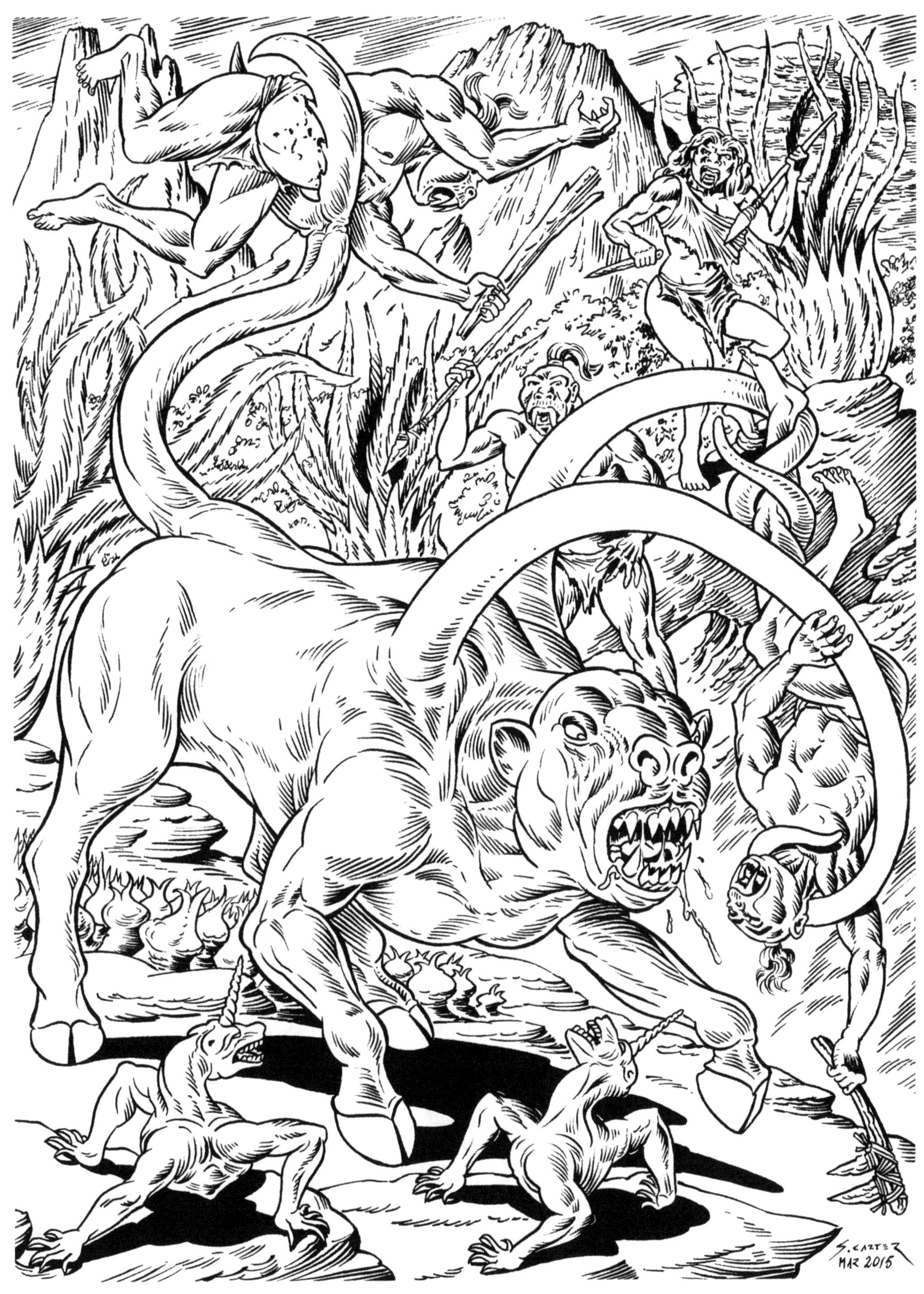

Peril of the Sabre-Tooth Clan
Illustration from "Alien Eden"

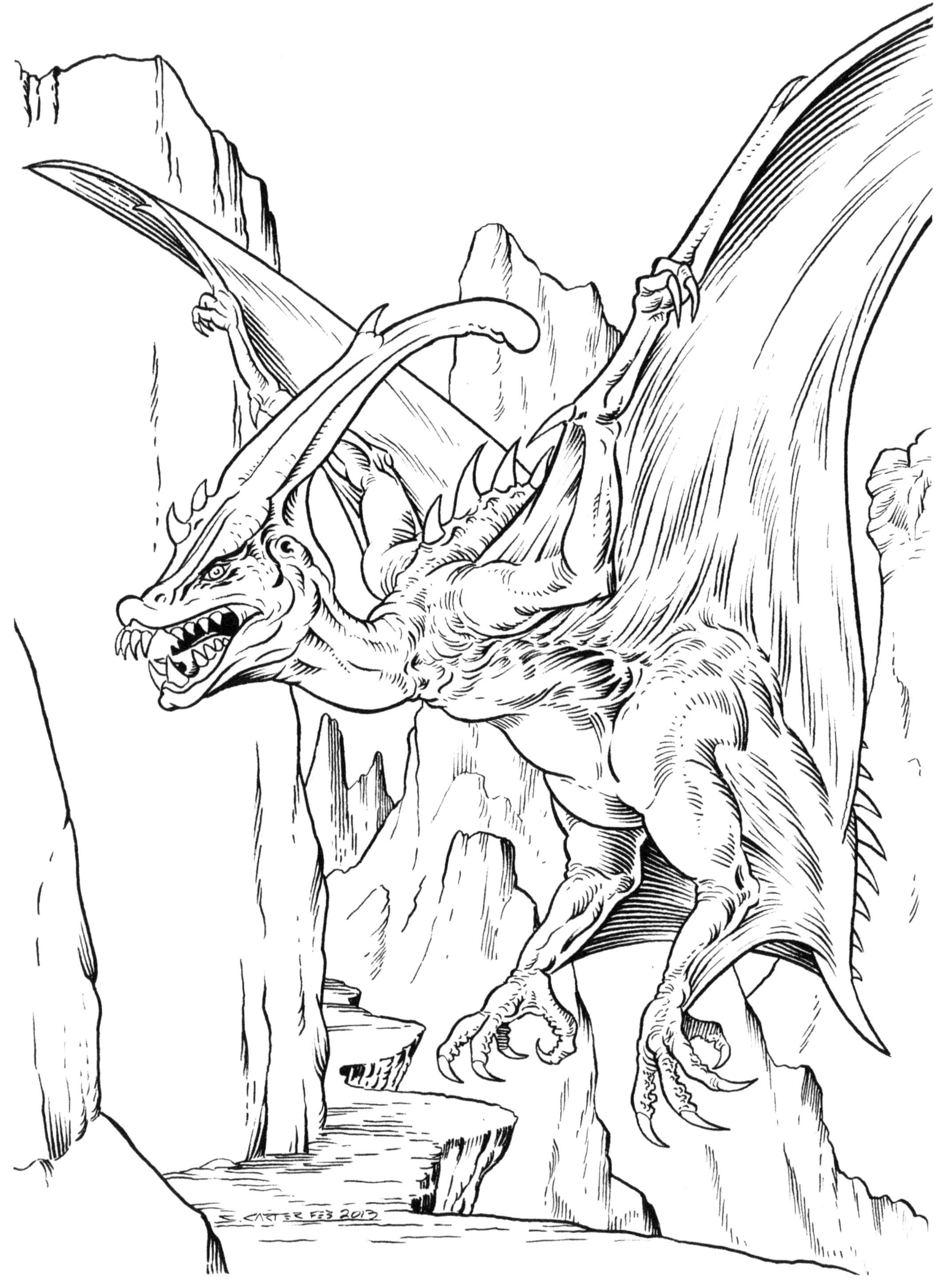

Pterosaurolophus

Illustration from "Weird Wild West 1: Hell Dorado"
by Carter Rydyr & Ethan Somerville

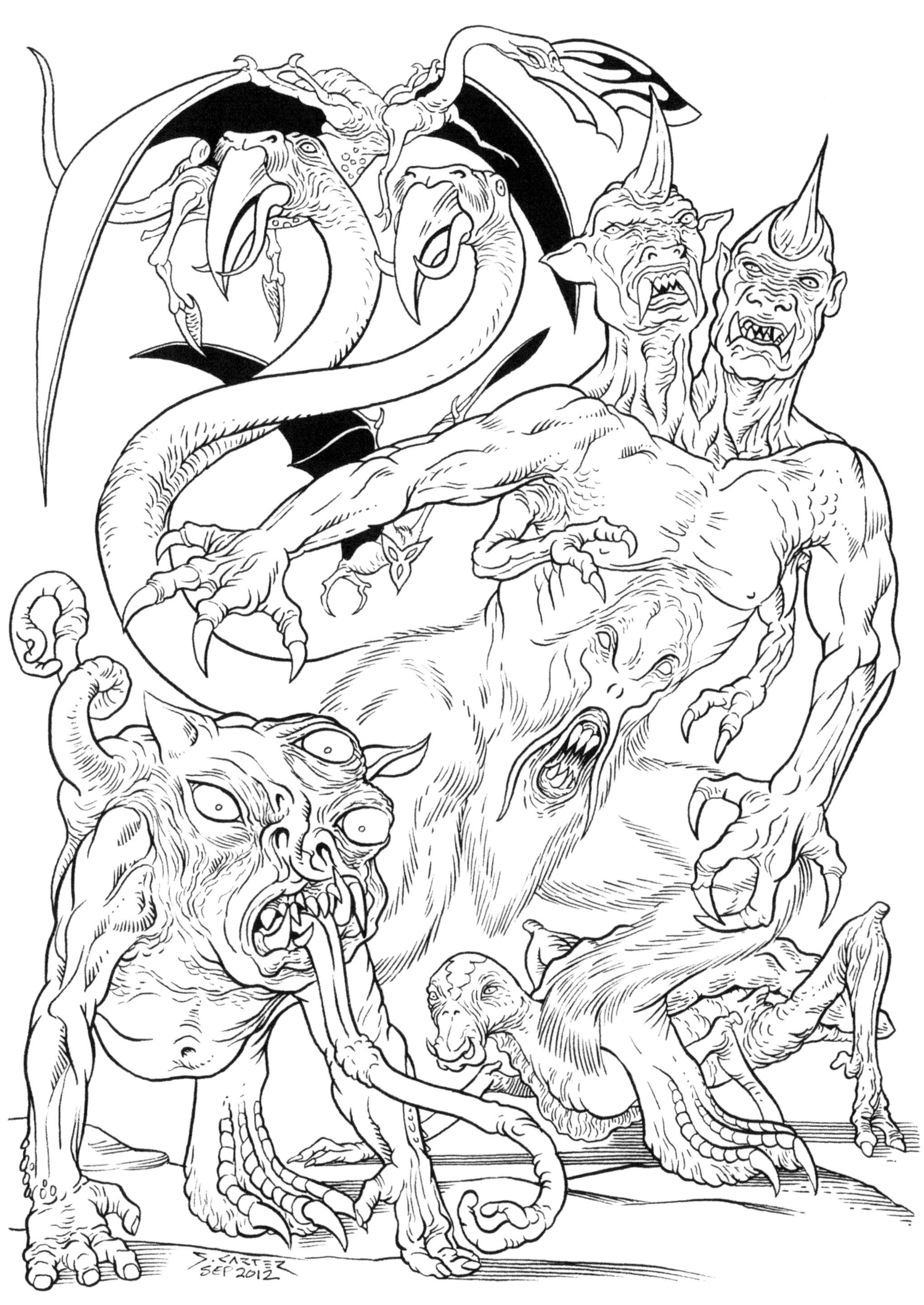

Random Anatomoids of the Morphysic Biosphere

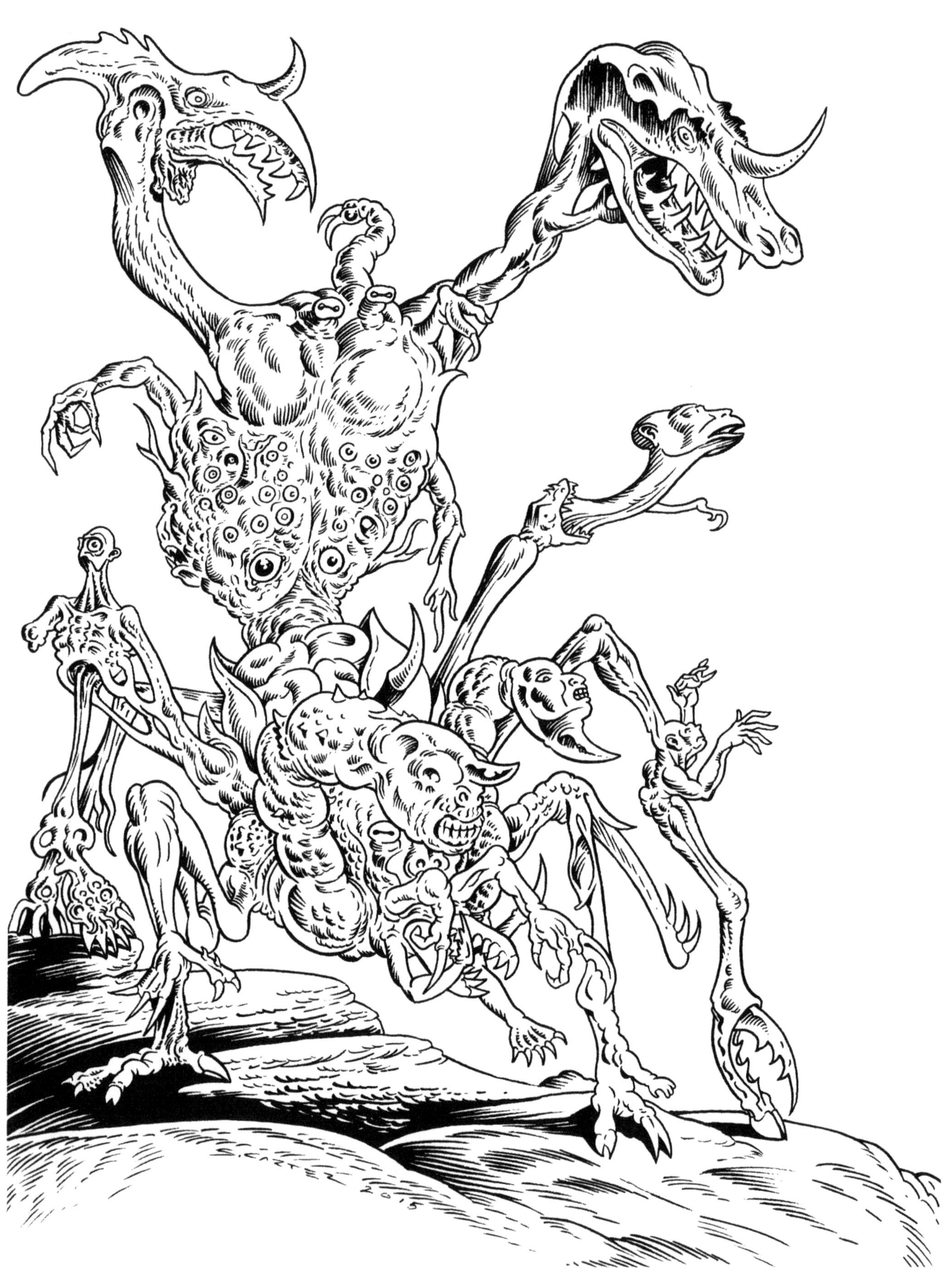

Random Genetic Monstrosity

Illustration from "Weird Wild West 6: The Monsters of Claiborne Manor" by Carter Rydyr & Ethan Somerville

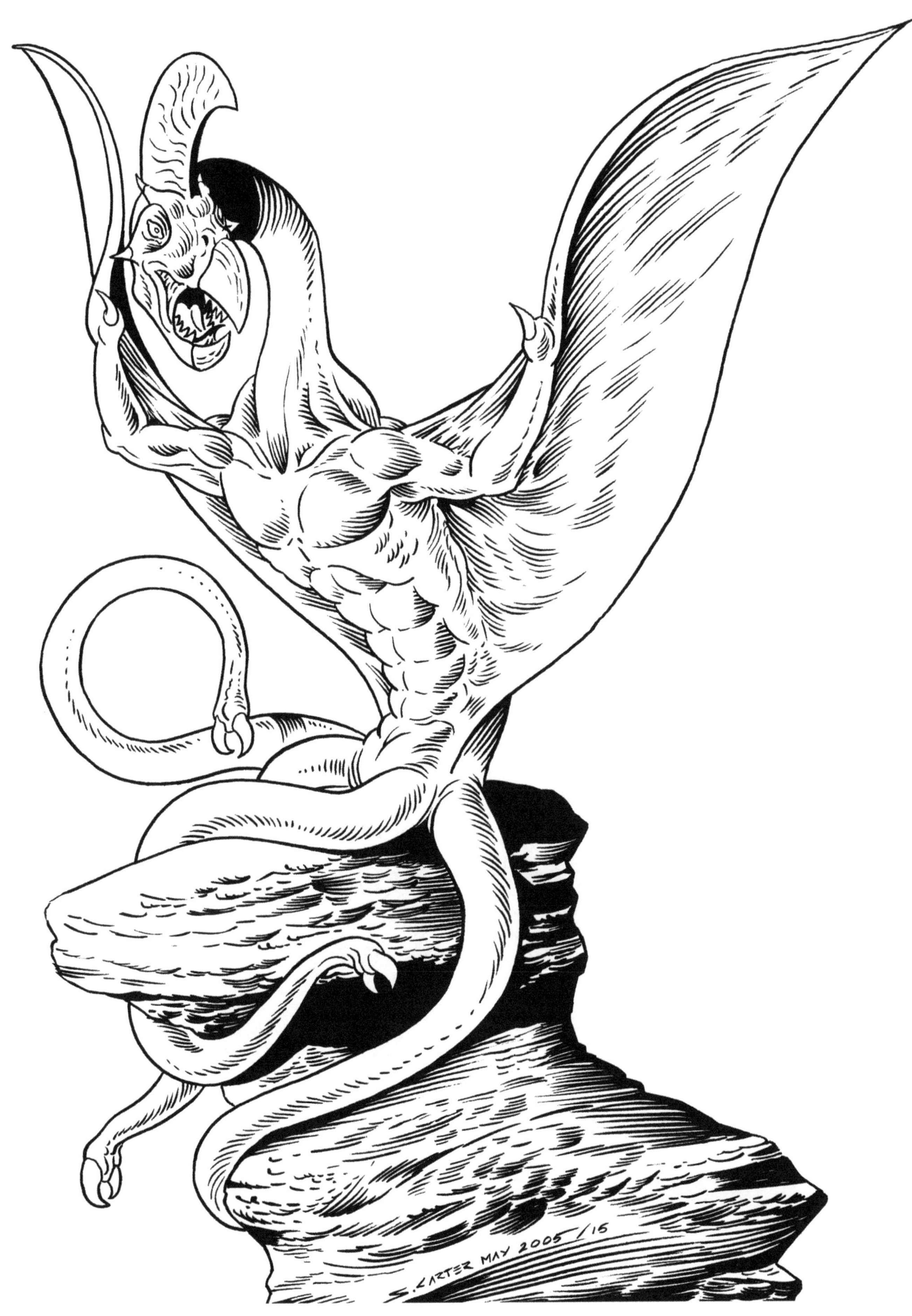

Nemesean Predatory Sky Strangler

Illustration from "Alien Eden"

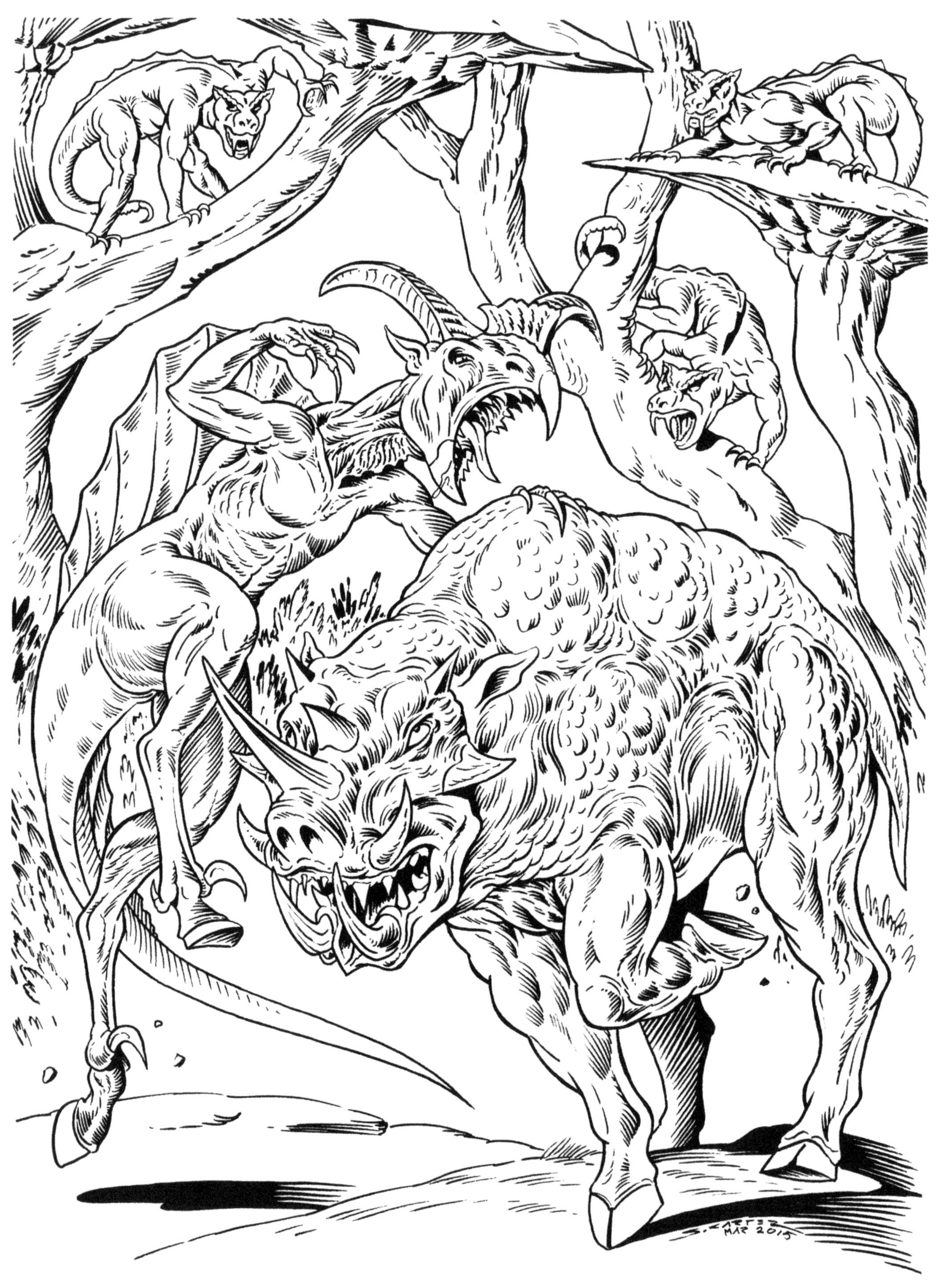

Conflict between a Rhinoboar ands a Sailbacked Raptor

Illustration from "Alien Eden"

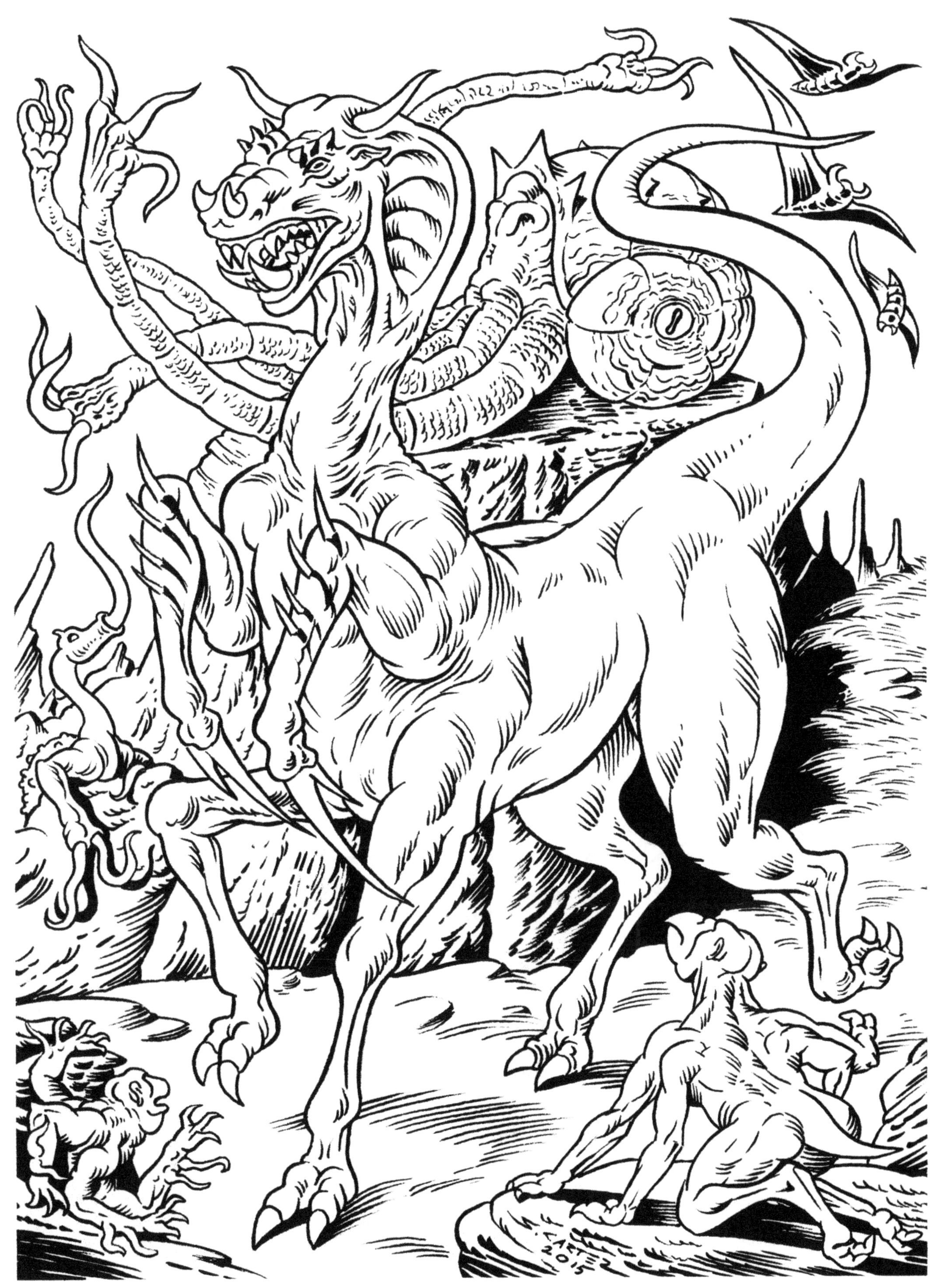

On The Road to Cuckoolu

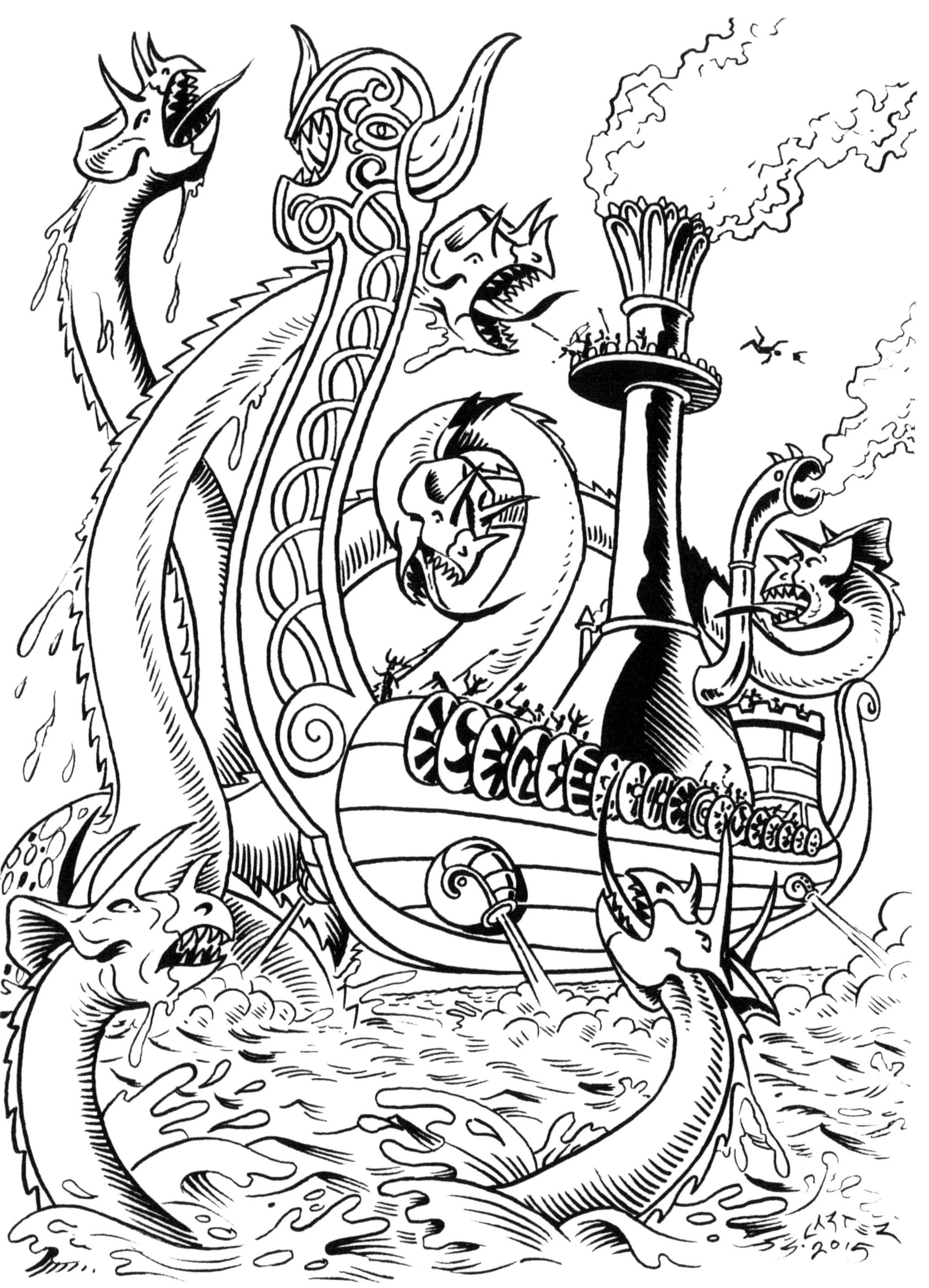

Sea Monster Mayhem

Illustration from "Weird Wild West 4: The Vyking War"
by Carter Rydyr & Ethan Somerville

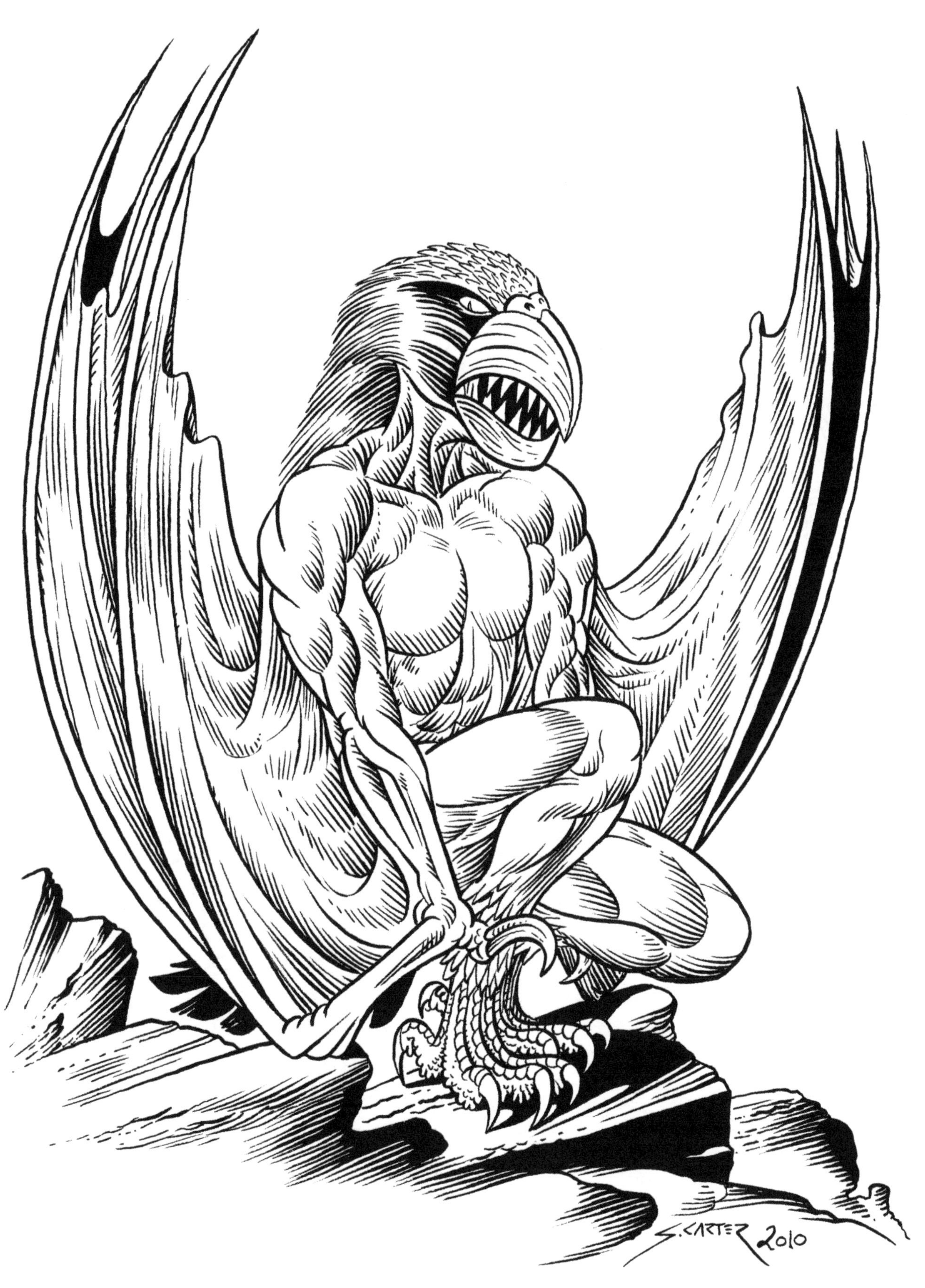

Terror Beaked Pterobat
Illustration from "Alien Eden"

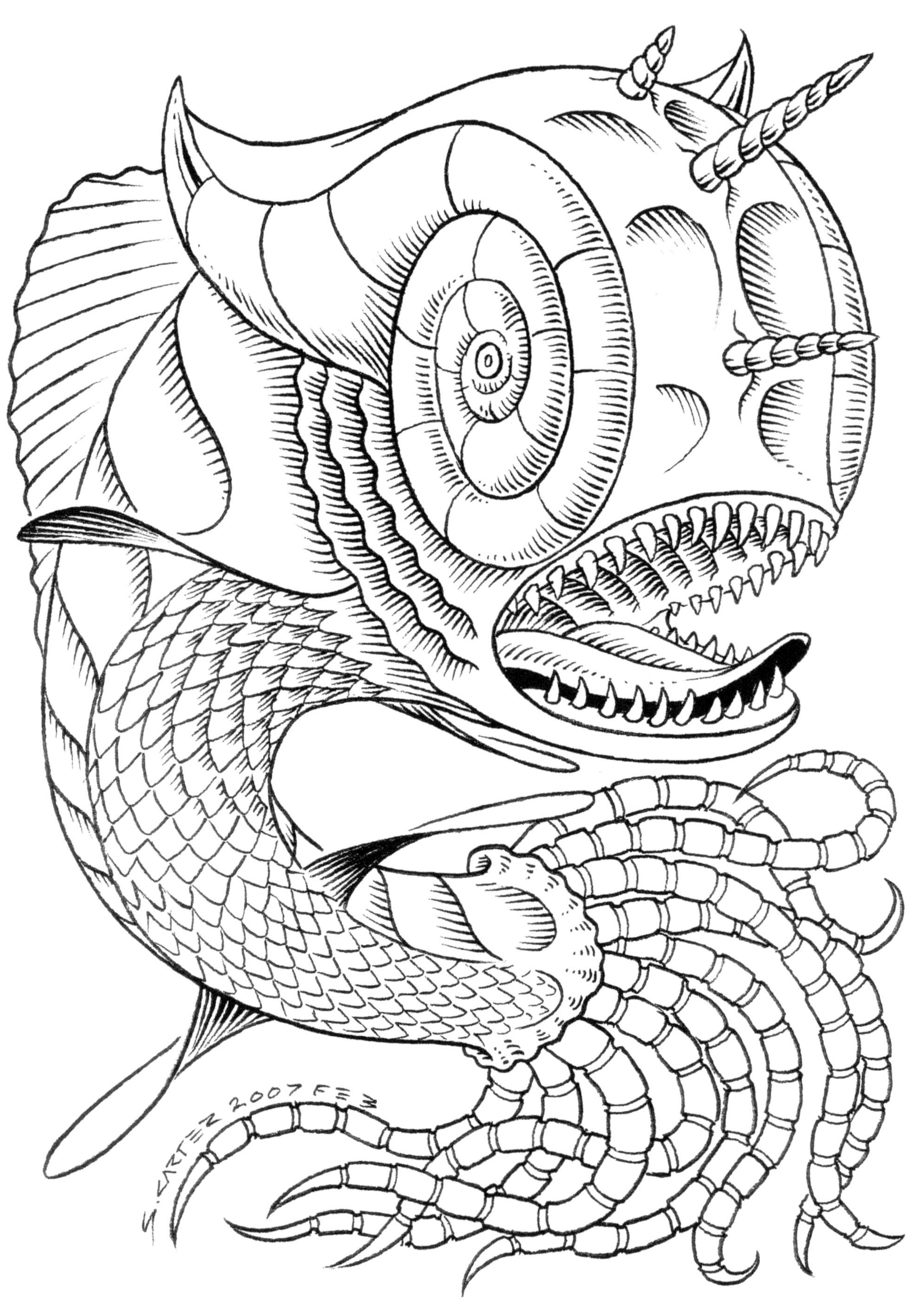

Armour Headed Dragon Fish
Illustration from "Alien Eden"

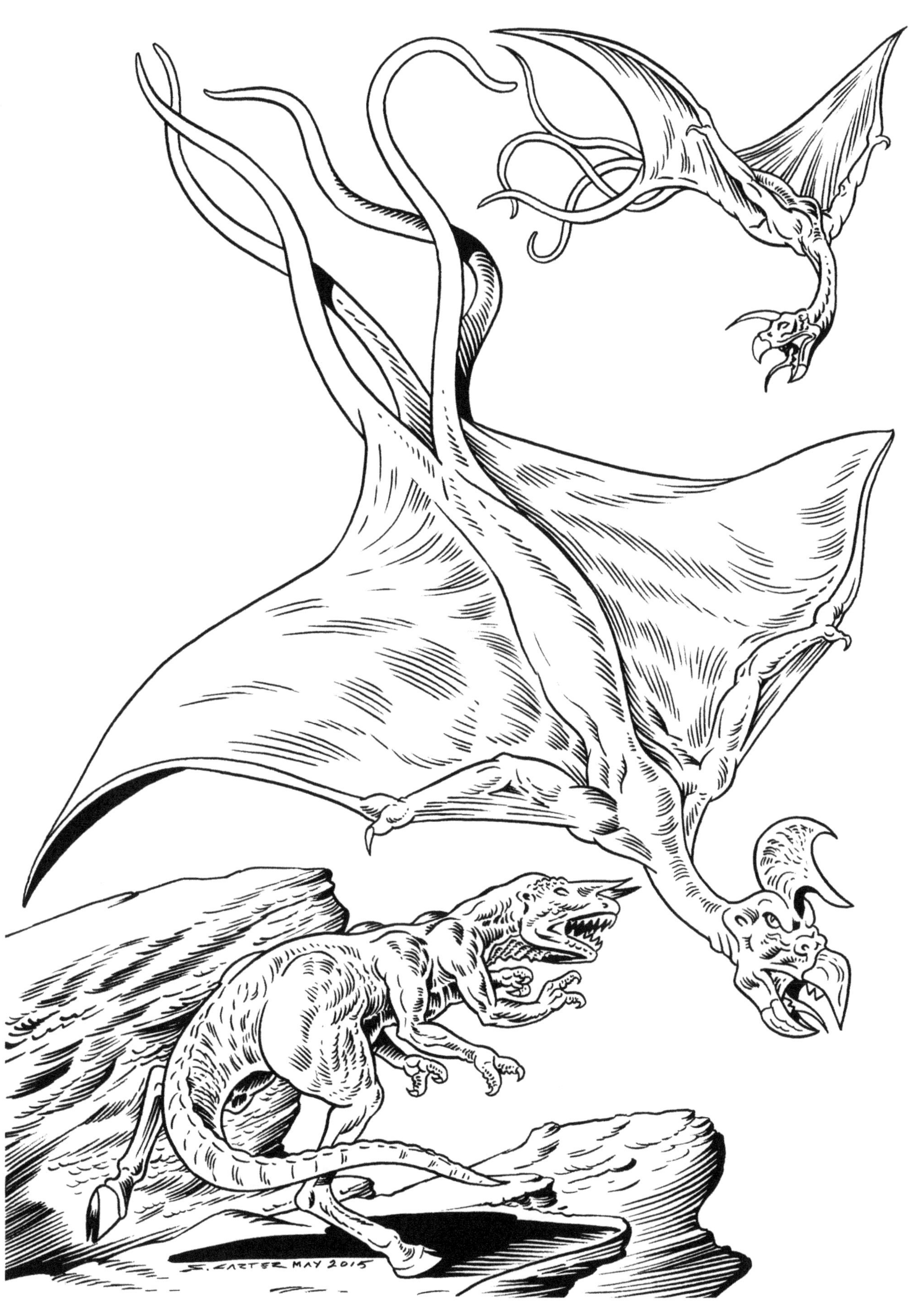

Squid Tailed Sky Stranglers swoop a Six-Limbed Saurian
Illustration from "Alien Eden"

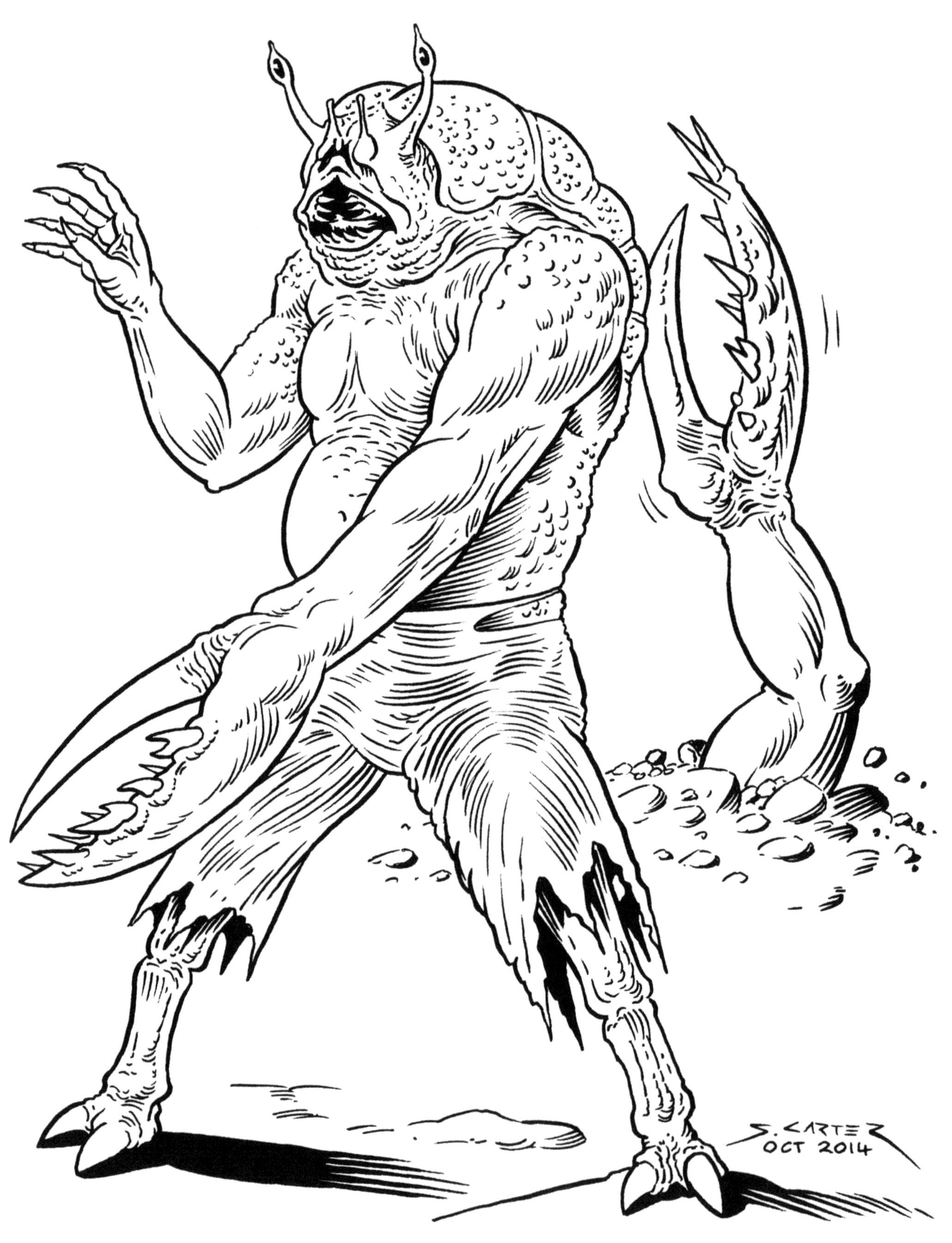

Subterranean Invaders
Illustration from "Weird Wild West 3: The Freaks of Mojo County"
by Carter Rydyr & Ethan Somerville

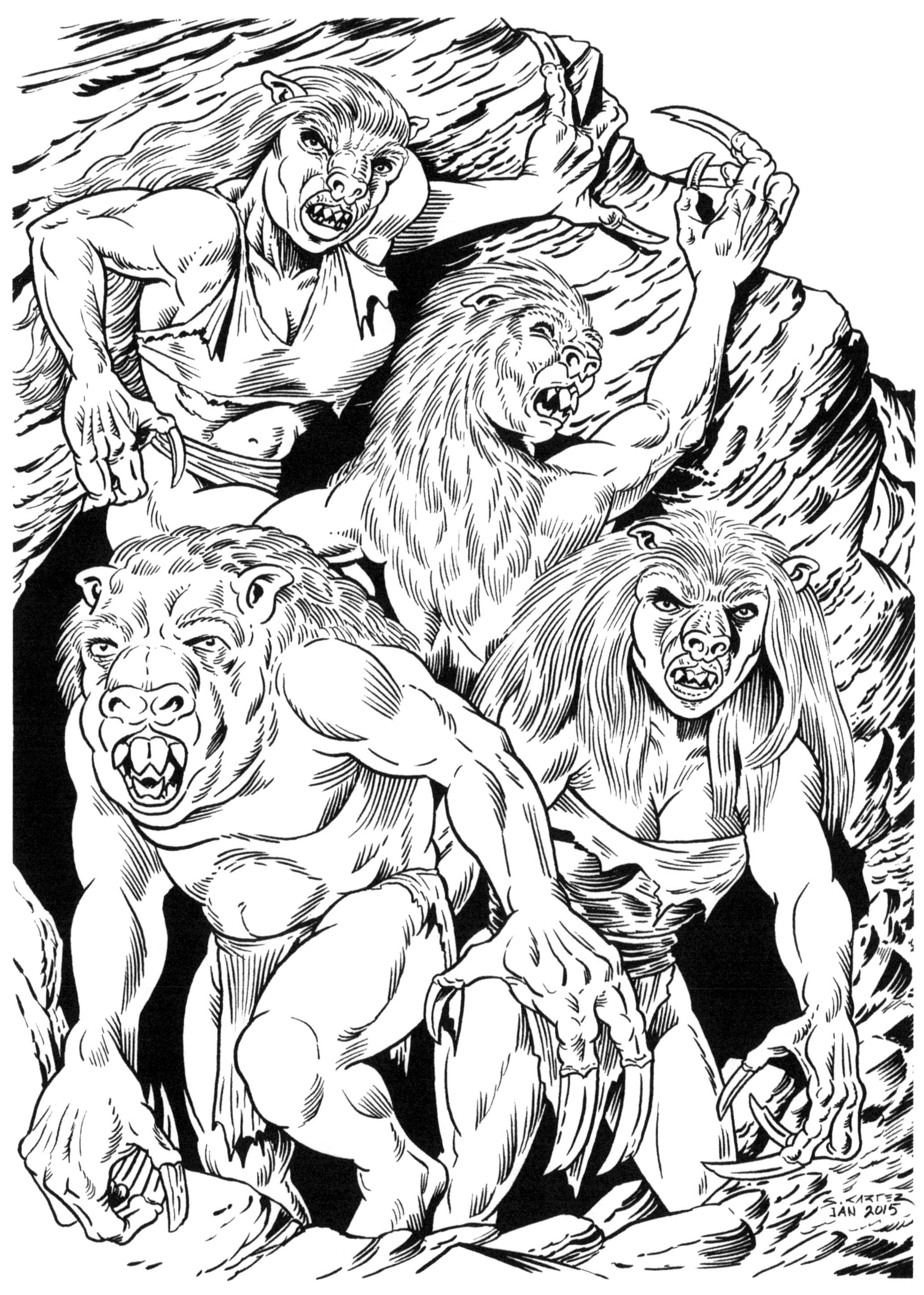

Trogons

Illustration from "Weird Wild West 4: The Vyking War"
by Carter Rydyr & Ethan Somerville

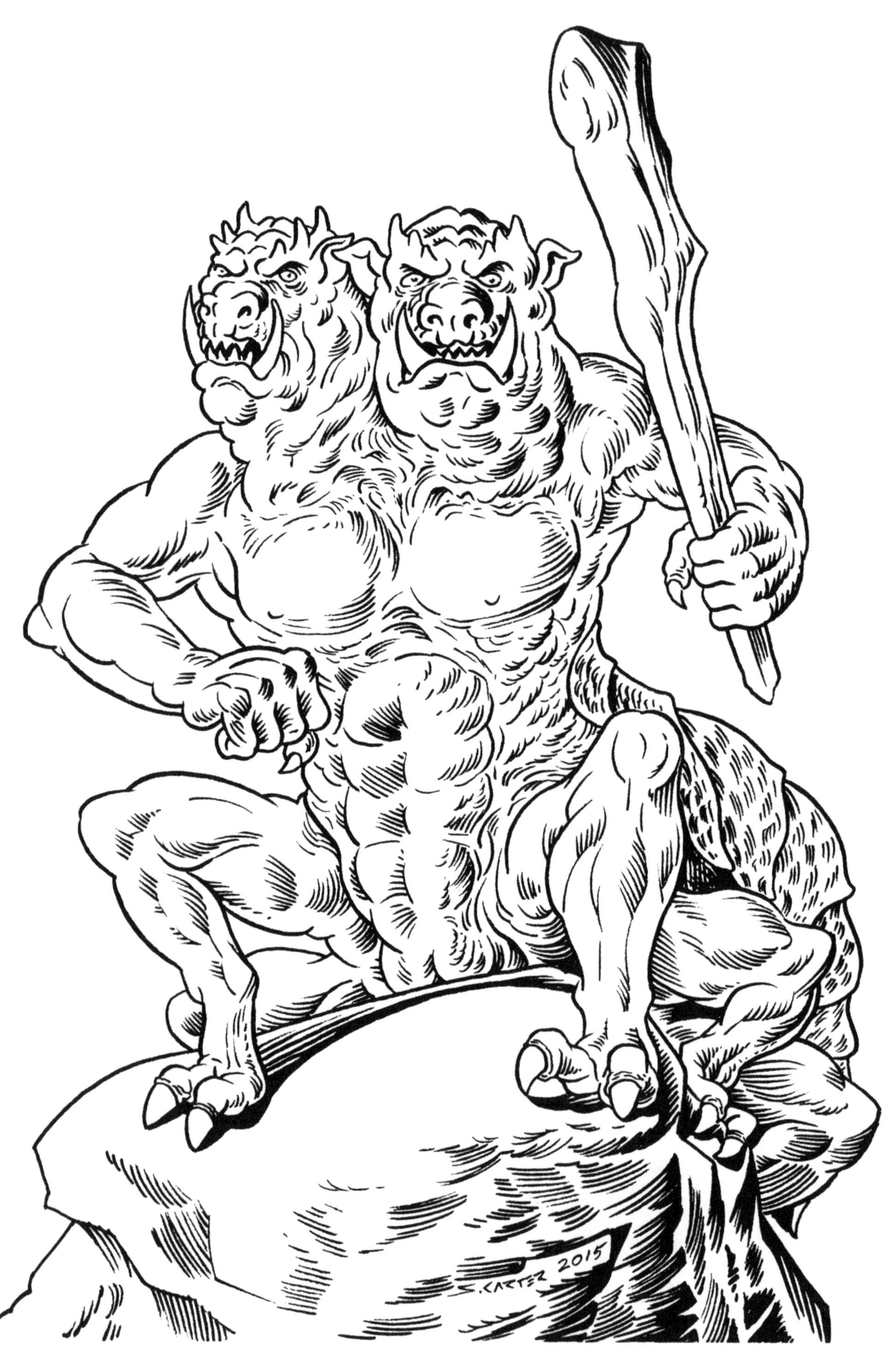

Two-Headed Trollabyte

Illustration from "Unworld - The World Before the Flood"

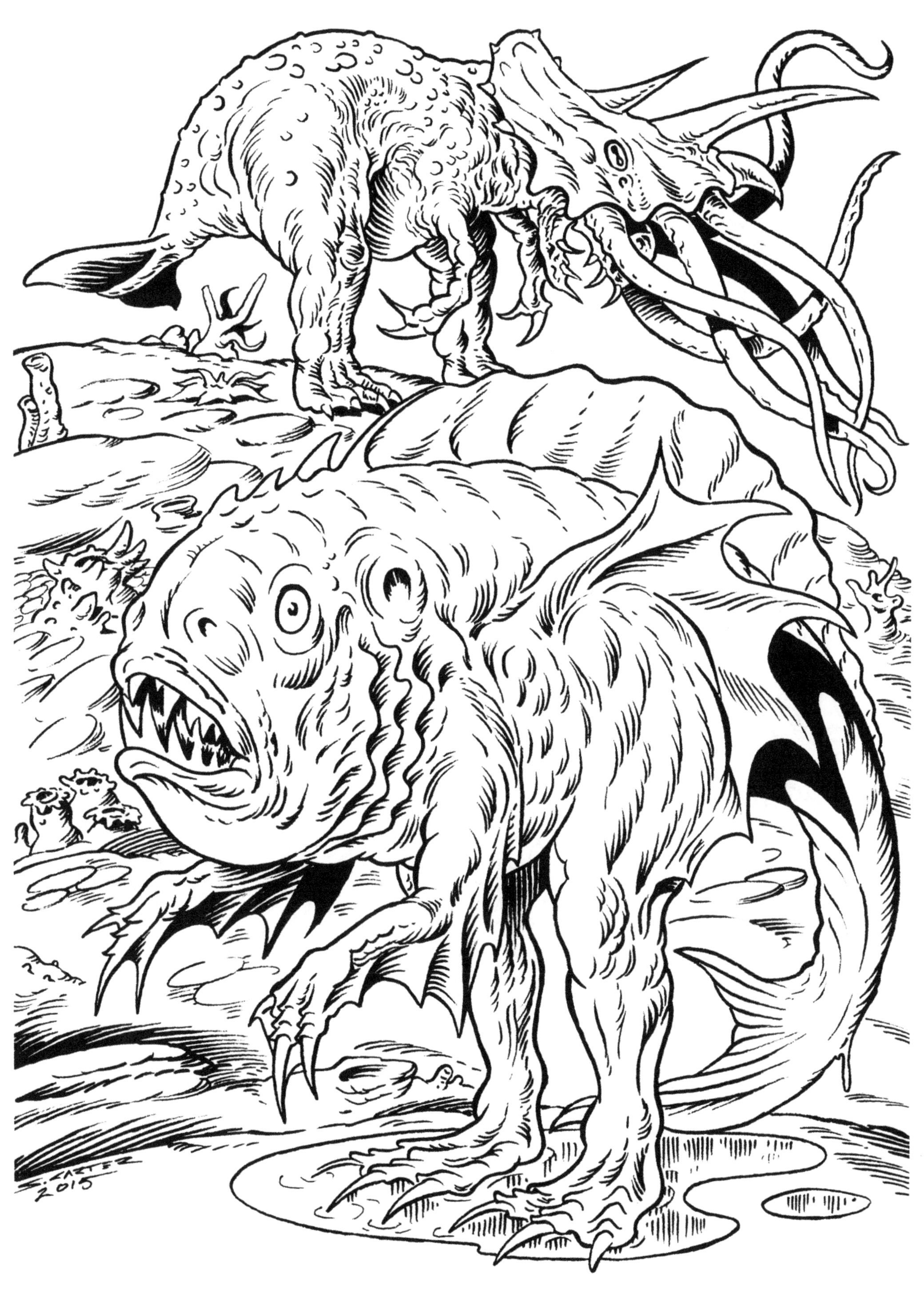

Dagonian Lifeforms

Illustration from "Alien Eden"

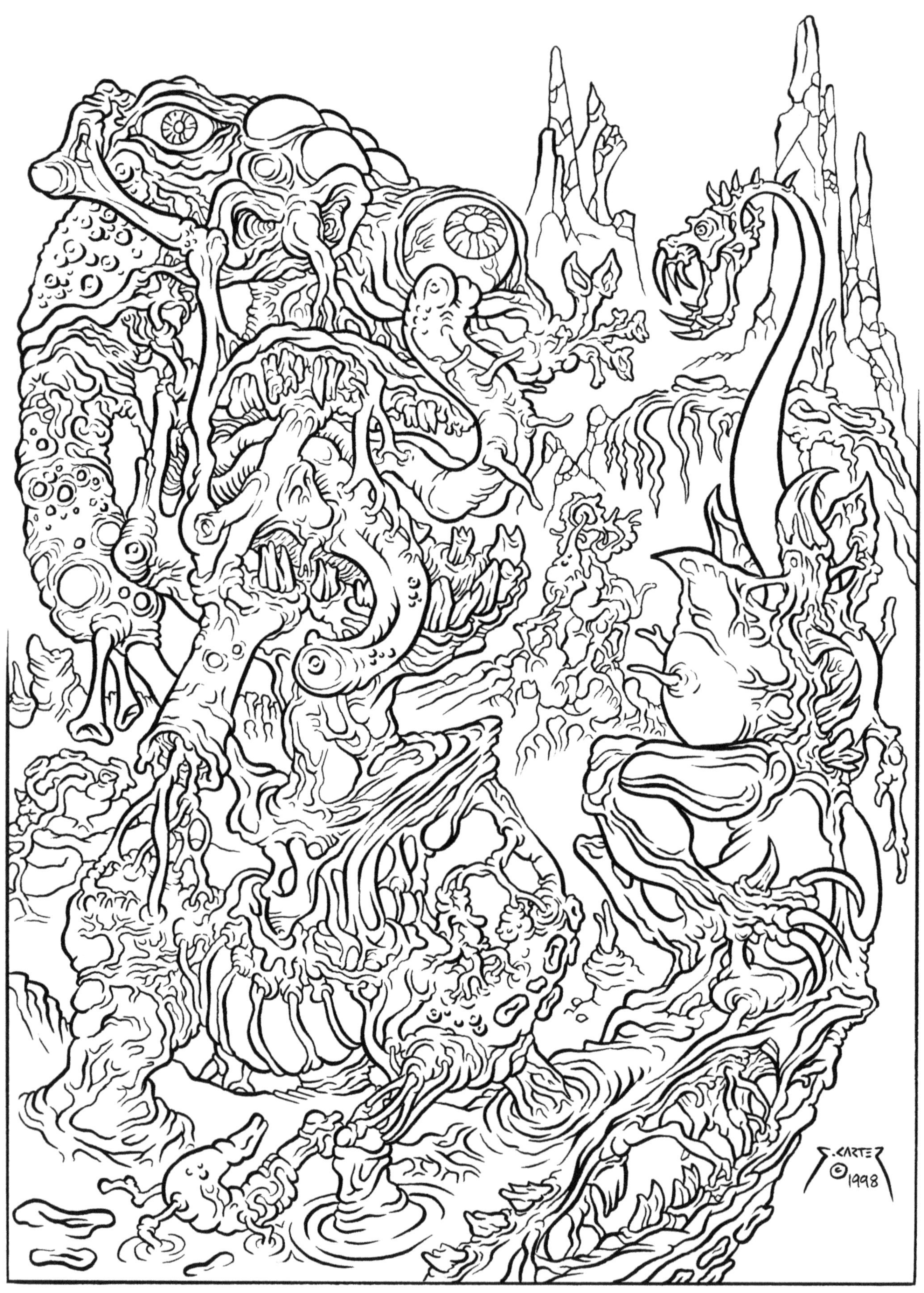

Evolutionary Mayhem

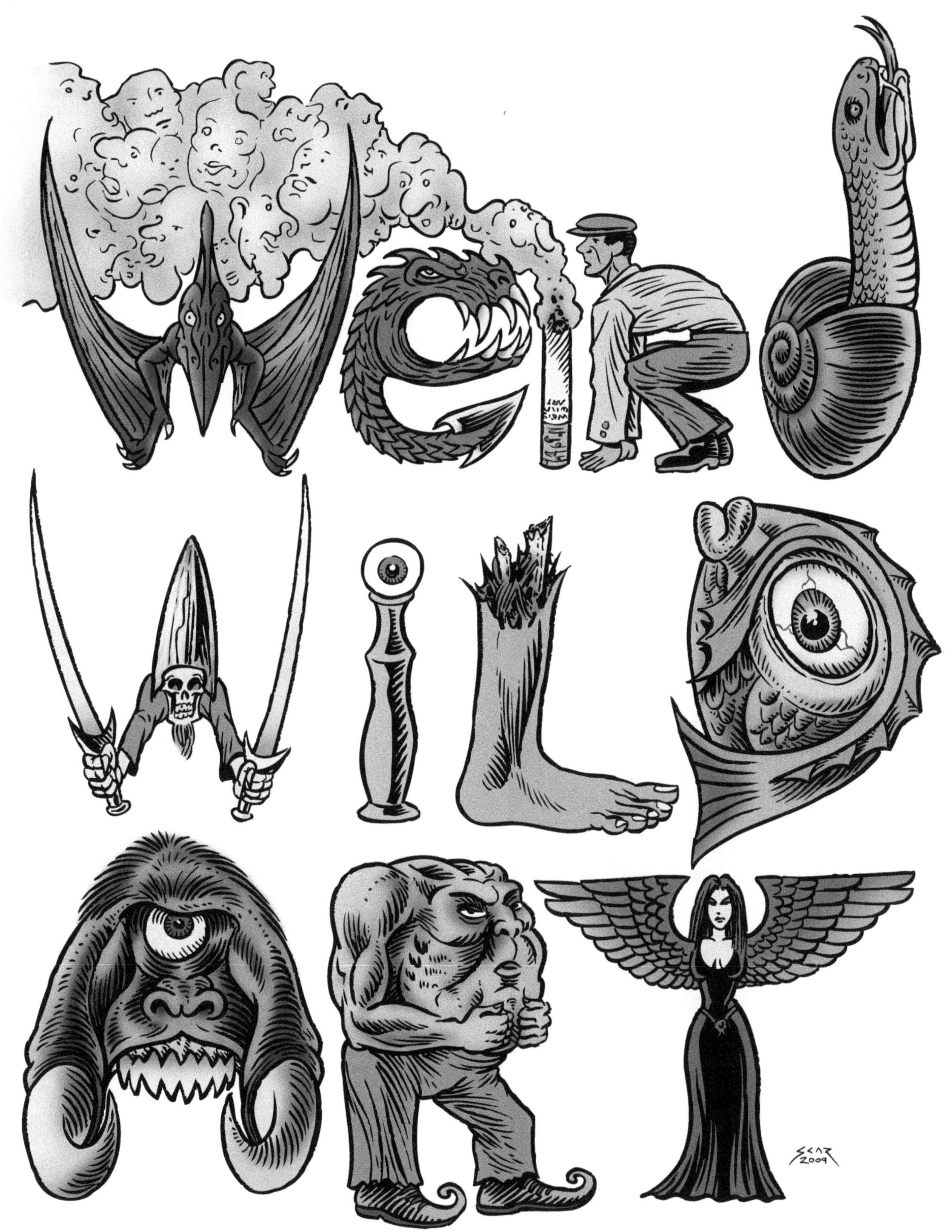

If you enjoyed this book by SCAR, have a look at their other titles and please consider writing a review. Thanks!

MORE BOOKS BY S.C.A.R.

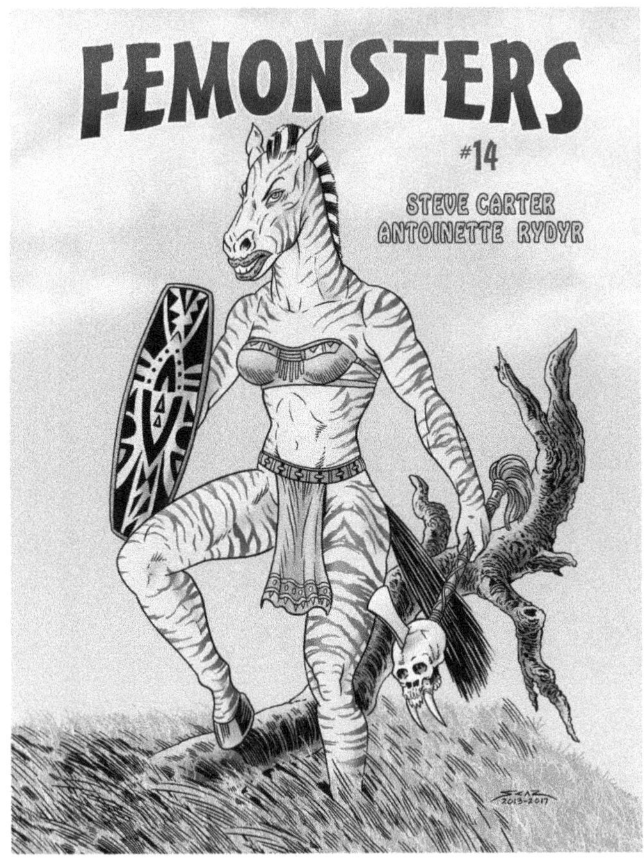

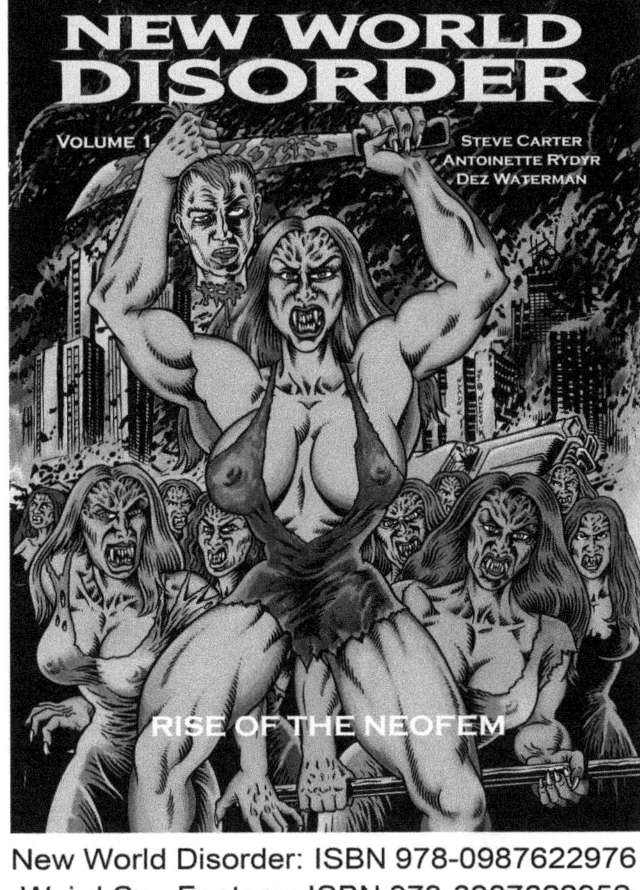

Femonsters #14: ISBN 978-0987622969
New World Disorder: ISBN 978-0987622976
Bestiary of Monstruum: ISBN 978-0987622945
Weird Sex Fantasy: ISBN 978-0987622952

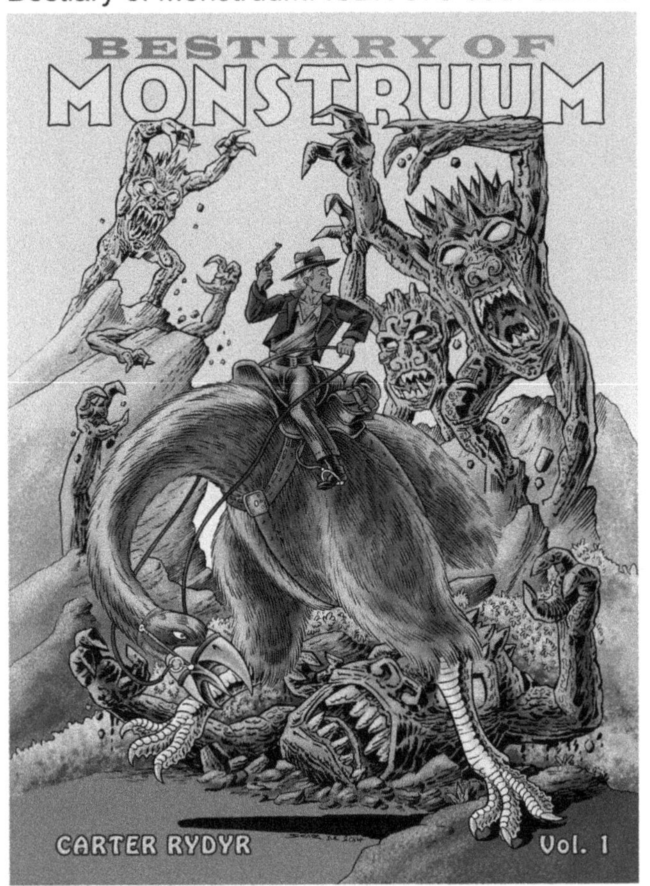

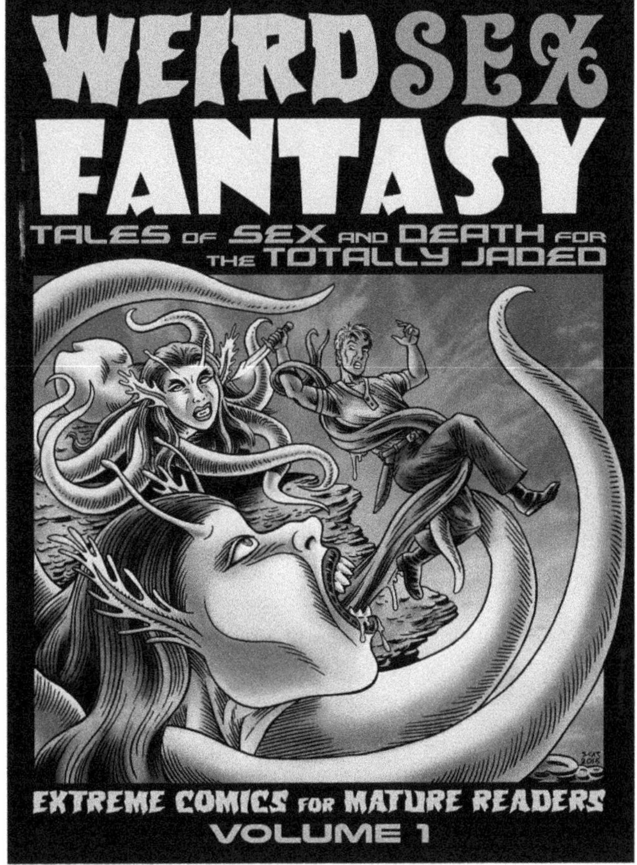

www.weirdwildart.com

CARTER RYDYR AND ETHAN SOMERVILLE

WEIRD WILD WEST

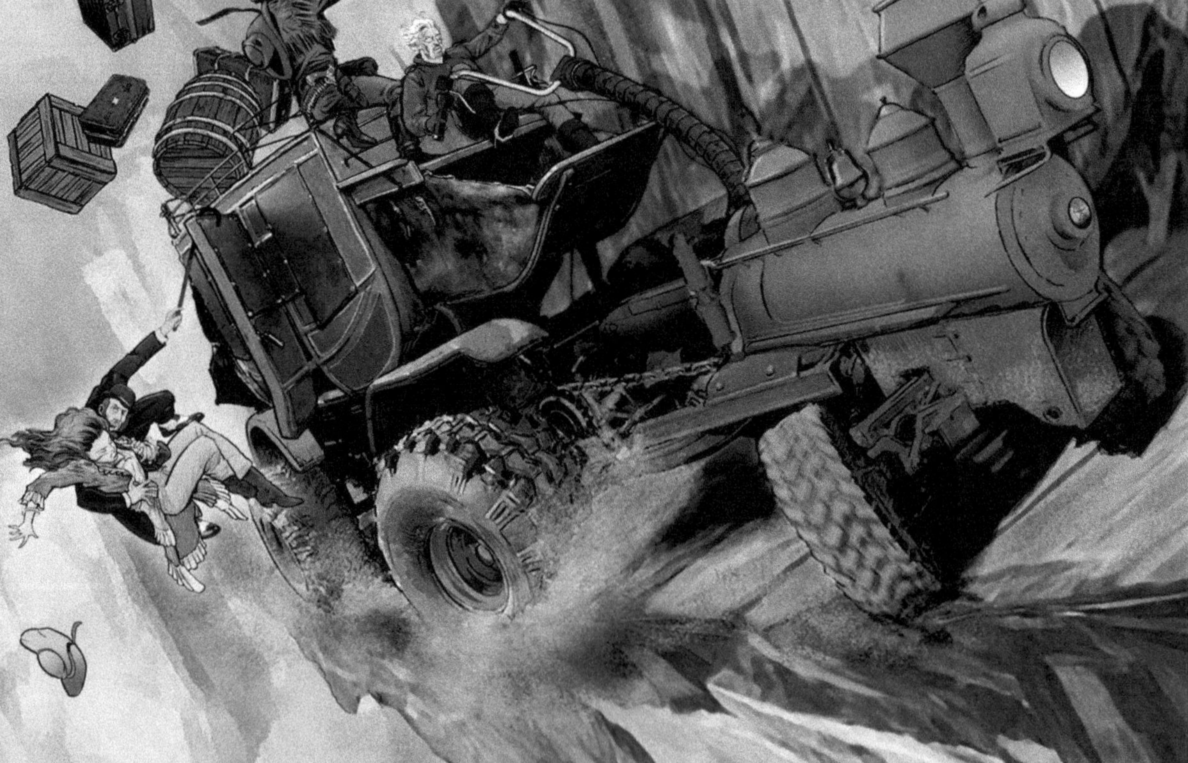

PART 1 – HELL DORADO

PART 2 – THE GOOD, THE BAD AND THE ZOMBIE

WEIRD WILD WEST

A New Novel by
Carter Rydyr
Ethan Somerville

Imagine a wild west that isn't just full of cowboys and outlaws, saloon girls and gamblers. Imagine a wild west that isn't just cacti, tumbleweeds and rolling desert as far as the eye can see. Imagine a wild west of mechanical horses, mutant killer plants, flying dinosaurs, headless indians and fearsome zombie gunslingers hell-bent on revenge.

Imagine the Weird Wild West.

Six colourful characters, some not entirely human, embark on a perilous journey south from Sunbleached Plains to Kellyville. A dapper dentist, a southern belle, a wealthy madam, a retired banker turned gambler, an orphaned boy and a travelling body-parts salesman all trade their various stories to pass the time.

Driving the carriage is one Zeke "the Freak" Sarandon, a retired soldier with more than one strange, nervous habit. Although he is an experienced traveller, and the only one insane enough to take the most direct route south, even he cannot prevent his passengers from each meeting their grisly demise, one by one.

Hot on the trail of the coach, astride an ancient mechanical horse blowing sparks and belching out toxic clouds of smoke, is a zombie gunslinger, the risen corpse of a murdered prospector.

For on the carriage is the one who killed him, and he must have his horrible, bloody revenge.

Bizarro Pulp Press
an imprint of JournalStone Publishing.

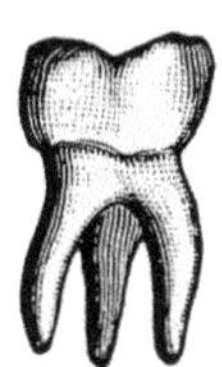

Published 2018
ISBN: 978-1-947654-40-2

www.ingramcontent.com/pod-product-compliance
Ingram Content Group UK Ltd.
Pitfield, Milton Keynes, MK11 3LW, UK
UKHW061830190726
13855UKWH00005B/1735